Susanne Peymann · Ingrid Kraaz von Rohr

Pendulum

Oracle · Advice · Counseling

Text by Susanne Peymann,
with a contribution by Ingrid Kraaz von Rohr

Translated from the German by Ulrich Magin

SHELTER HARBOR PRESS
NEW YORK

Pendulum

Contents

List of the pendulum diagrams

Using the Pendulum –
spiritually and practically

Contact with higher forces
and deeper layers of consciousness

One of the most commonly used oracles is the pendulum. It is related to water divining as well as to physics and modern art. There are many interesting myths about dowsers and their use of the pendulum, but if you delve deeper you will understand that the pendulum brings real results. From modern physics to psychology, from New Age to art, the pendulum, as well as dowsing, is a part of our culture and history. Umberto Eco's famous novel *Foucault's Pendulum* is an excellent interpretation of the pendulum and its cultural context.

There is another very popular modern novel which has depicted the power of the pendulum with the use of fascinating metaphors – Momo, by Michael Ende. In the novel, the girl, *Momo,* accompanied by Master Hora, enters the place where time originates, over which breaks a golden dawn, with the view of an enormous, round celestial dome on the skyline. From an opening in the center of this dome, a column of light vertically falls on a circular and dark pond. "Close to the surface of the water, something glittered in this column of light like a brilliant star", we read (German edition, 1978, p. 161), "and Momo was able to discern an enormous pendulum, swinging to and fro above the jet black mirror."

Each swing of this pendulum creates a flower of extraordinary beauty, fragrance, and sound, while, at the same time, another flower withers. Each swing of the pendulum creates a new and precious flower, yet none of these flowers resemble any other, in keeping with the pendulum, which never touches the same place on a surface twice.

Momo has been a witness to the "flowers of the hour" and the "star pendulum" and has experienced this momentary beauty which Master Hora *(hora,* Lat.: clock, hour) watches over. This pendulum of

XXI

ᚱ The Universe ♄

The card "XXI–The Universe" from the Tarot of Lady Frieda Harris and Aleister Crowley. "A dancer with one foot on a serpent's head. At the center of the image a body in equilibrium. Pendulum and sickle depict the quality of time. All in all, it is also an image of the eternal golden braid of evolution, of the development from simply being into being aware. – Pendulum and sickle: as clockwork and instrument of harvest they symbolize quality and quantity of time, even our own part in eternity." (E. Bürger / J. Fiebig).

Master Hora emphasizes the higher forces that determine our lives. The impressive experiment with the pendulum by Léon Foucault (see p. 10) made higher forces visible in a similar way. This is still one of the most significant aspects of working with the pendulum today.

On the other hand, we need to take the pendulum into our own hands and hold it tight. This stresses our own initiative and responsibility when working with the pendulum, the need to find our inner balance and contact the deeper layers of our consciousness.

Taking inner unrest into your hands, and finding peace

As long as we live, we are constantly in movement. We never really stand still, we are constantly and perpetually in movement. At the same time, when we become conscious of this inner unrest and perpetual movement, particularly by means of the pendulum, we will generally experience peace and quiet. Even the pure act of using the pendulum can relax us and lead to inner meditation.

Small wonder, then, that the classic hypnotic therapies (which were still common practice at the time of Freud in the early 20th century) worked with the power of the pendulum. We have all seen this in movies or read about it in novels: an object, a pocket watch for example, being swung to and fro in front of a person's eyes in order to hypnotize him or her. The uniformity of this movement of the pendulum is a method for finding rest, to lower the threshold of our consciousness, helping the transgression into sleep or into a day-dreaming, trance-like state.

This resembles the feeling we can experience whilst lying in bed, when we feel we are leaving ourselves to another dimension where we do not really know what will happen. A similar situation is when we awake in a darkened room and immediately open our eyes to see something that we do not recognize at first, even though we are in our own room. It takes some time – which may seem to last a while, although it is no more than a fraction of a second – until we recognize things for what they are, and it takes even longer until we see the

Foucault's pendulum

Beginning in 1851, the French physicist Jean Bernard Léon Foucault repeated an experiment several times, in front of large audiences, which had originally been conducted by Vincenzo Viviani (1661), a pupil of Galileo Galilei.

He had a large, heavy pendulum which swung on a long rope in high rooms. While the pendulum, due to its high overhead suspension, always swings in the same place, the ground below the pendulum turns slowly. This renders the rotation of the Earth visible; and this can be easily perceived, even by laymen.

During his public experiments in the observatory and in the Panthéon of Paris, Foucault equipped his pendulum at the lower end with a point which drew a trace into the sand at the ground with each rotation.

Today, you can see this experiment as a reconstruction in many museums. The point of the pendulum draws a circular diagram in the shape of a flower's petals into the sand. The beauty of cosmic movement is clearly there for all to see.

A FOUCAULT'S PENDULUM IN THE ORANGERY, IN KASSEL, GERMANY.

objects in the forms and meanings we know well. In these situations, the moment appears prolonged as though in slow motion, and, at the same time, more intense than usual, as we experience a lot in very little time!

When using the pendulum, two aspects help create this meditative mood: firstly, our preparation for dowsing with the pendulum – we should connect with the earth, relax and empty our mind from all expectation and prejudice; secondly, the act of using the pendulum in itself as a form of self-hypnosis (deep mediation).

To summarize: When using the pendulum, we come into contact with higher forces and, at the same time, with the deeper layers of our very existence and our personality. The invisible becomes visible.

Using the pendulum in radiesthesia

The objective of radiesthesia is the searching for and finding of hidden or lost objects, or subterranean deposits of resources or other materials. Most well-known is water divining to find underground water veins. For many people who use the pendulum, the pendulum or tensor, the one-hand rod and other "instruments of the mind" are the instruments of choice.

The art of radiesthesia (a Latin-Greek word which means "perception of rays") is usually categorized into two sections. *"Physical radiesthesia* investigates material objects such as minerals, metals, plants or the bodies of living beings. It takes it as a given that all physical objects are based on frequencies. One of the founders of physical radiesthesia is the physicist Reinhard Schneider who, in 1951, invented the Lecher rod. This Lecher rod, based on the Lecher conductor, is the main instrument of physical radiesthesia", as the German edition of the web encyclopedia Wikipedia puts it. The German version continues:

"**Mental radiesthesia analyzes subtle phenomena such as, for example, energy bodies or so-called 'influences from a distance'. One also finds terms like** *odic radiesthesia* **(investigations of the aura) and** *psychic radiesthesia* **(investigations of the human psyche), but both are classed as mental radiesthesia today. […] The instrument used in radiesthesia is the divining rod, which was first documented in the Middle Ages. Meanwhile, other forms like the one-hand-rod (also called tensor) and the Lecher rod are being used. Some people prefer to use the pendulum. The process of detection by these instruments is called 'divining in radiesthesia'."**

Historical sources

The Etruscans and Romans had several oracle-like rituals which were carried out by different instruments. Among these was the *lituus* (a crooked stave which was used to make important political or military decisions or to locate places where something should be built), the *aquilegus* (a stave used to find water veins) and the *anulus* (a ring made of metal or plant fiber which was used to divine the future), which is a precursor of our pendulum.

These rituals, the execution of which was reserved to the class of priests in Roman times, turned into popular methods of folk divination during the Middle Ages, for example in "turning the sieve" or "making the stave jump". During the Renaissance these practices became the subject of theoretical speculation: it was assumed that the rod of a water diviner or dowser was influenced by subterranean demons. Other theories reckoned with certain "corpuscula" (tiny particles) which were emitted by the substance being searched for, and which were caught by the rod, stave, or pendulum.

Today, we may smile or even shake our heads at such naivety. However, at a time when nothing was yet known about radio waves, other waves or rays, such concepts certainly expressed the best ideas about the existence and effects of such invisible forces.

Boom in the "Pluto"-years

The internet encyclopedia Wikipedia has this to report about the history of radiesthesia: "In the middle of the 19th century, the Vienna neurologist and university professor Moriz Benedikt used diving rods to locate 'pathogenic places' he assumed were the cause of diseases and illnesses [pathogenic means: causing disease]. In 1929, the German natural scientist Gustav Freiherr von Pohl first described his ideas about earth rays. He assumed that there were subterranean water veins which emitted a kind of radiation that was harmful to people, animals, and plants. This would go right through the soil and could be detected by people who were especially sensitive and gifted, the

radiesthesists. Between 1930 and 1945, this 'ray detection' was at its zenith, the Abbé Alexis Timothée Bouly, in his work *La Radiesthésie ou comment devenir expert...*, published around 1931, coined the term 'radiesthesia'. In addition, the word 'geopathy' was used for the alleged unhealthy effects of certain places."

These are certainly interesting ideas. The years of the Second World War, as well as the years around 1930 when the planet Pluto was discovered, were a very important period for the genesis of modern radiesthesia.

Pluto was discovered on 18 February 1930. The name refers to the Greek-Roman god Pluto. It has two mythological identities: Pluto Nr 1 (also Pluton or Hades) is the god of the underworld. Hades, in Greek, means "He who can't be perceived", and when Hades visits earth, he often wears his cloak of invisibility. Pluto Nr 2 (also called Plutos), the little fellow with the cornucopia who accompanies the deity of destiny, Tyche (Latin: Fortuna), donates happiness and blessings. He is the god of plenty and wealth, especially wealth that stems from the ground.

The discovery of Pluto (which is no longer considered a major planet as it is too small) is characteristic of an era that saw hell open its gates in the form of the Second World War, but that also saw the laying of the foundations for positive opportunities such as wealth and human rights for nations all over the world. In the past, these had been slumbering in the unconscious or unknown. This era, when plutonic forces emerged on the threshold of consciousness, also marks the time in which modern dowsing with rods as well as the use of the pendulum experienced their zenith. The pendulum had a new and fresh renaissance as a modern oracle with its "esoteric trends", beginning in the late 20th century, as did several other disciplines.

In brief: As a celestial body, Pluto was discovered on 18 February 1930. February 18, according to astrological definitions, is a day when the zodiacal sign of Aquarius crosses into the zodiacal sign of Pisces; a common interpretation of the sign of Aquarius is "I know", and a common definition of the sign of Pisces reads: "I believe". In other words, "Just at the very place where knowledge ends and faith begins, in the 20th century we discover the subterranean, shadowy mega forces of Pluto with their extreme aspects of destruction and healing" (Johannes Fiebig). It is exactly these forces which have also encouraged the current boom of radiesthesia.

Divining

Whether you are more interested in "physical" or "mental" (spiritual) radiesthesia, you need an instrument for your investigations. Of those available, the pendulum is the most widespread and the most practical, as it needs little space and is not too exposed to exterior influences.

Using the pendulum is not difficult. Before you start, you need to define a personal way or code in which you may interpret the rotations or straight movements of the pendulum as a positive or negative response. Then you always need to proceed in strict keeping to this code (see p. 36).

After you've defined what you are about to search for (a liquid, an object, a person, a disease etc.), you need to relate to it and form a question in your mind which may be answered by a simple yes or no, such as "Is it here?" or "Is this it?".

You may encounter further answers from the number of the times the pendulum turns or from its frequencies, and you need to determine in advance that a certain number of rotations signify a certain distance, an amount, a number of days, years or something else.

"We should not steer too quickly towards our objective," Roberto Gadini writes and continues: "Radiesthesia is a mental discipline, and to become competent seekers we cannot refrain from closing in on all hints […] gradually, step by step."

Many things become easier once we understand that the use of the divining rod or of the pendulum has nothing to do with the "supernatural", rather it encourages an enhancement and a refinement of our senses.

A part of the success on our way to become a pendulum practitioner is the increasing ability to differentiate between a thing or sign on the one hand and the personal, relevant meaning of it for us on the other hand. An underground water vein or stream, for example, the most important and also most often used target of investigation in classic radiesthesia, may have quite different practical implications (see text on following page).

The localization of hidden substances and sources of rays with a pendulum and a divining rod is called dowsing or divining. There may be sources of interference which we need to discover in order to switch them off or to release them. Yet there may also be hidden treasures which have attracted us unconsciously, because we have thought about them but not known them consciously …

In divining, we get to the bottom of the divine. We need courage to follow our own inspiration and insights and frequencies. And we need the strength to differentiate between mere appearance and true meaning.

Subterranean water veins – what they imply

A real underground water vein may be regarded as an environmental source of interference. However, if we become conscious of its power and adapt to it, we may change its effect and find it relaxing and invigorating.

In addition to the material circumstances a subterranean water vein or stream may have a symbolic meaning that is no less real. An underground stream is a subterranean river, which means a river that is hidden from our view, something which exists but is active in the unknown or hidden, like, for example:

- the river of life and the ravages of time: in a way, the "biological clock" which always runs;
- the river of life and of our (own) vitality, our (own) time which may appear lost or which has not been uncovered or born;
- our own concerns that have been lost, buried, cannot be reached or haven't yet emerged and developed;
- a lost, unknown or unredeemed concern may, in our daily routine, make us feel unwell, irritated or molested.

Once you start looking for a "subterranean water vein" as a cause for this condition, you may well do rightly so. But this "subterranean water vein" may be more of a symbol than an actual flow of water.

The Story of the Youth Who Went Forth to Learn What Fear Was In many fairy tales, we learn about the destructive and life-giving qualities of water. A father had two sons, the younger of which simply could not understand anything. His greatest desire was to learn what fear is. He starts to explore, thinking, "if only I could learn to shudder with fear!" He spends a night beneath the gallows with seven hanged men still hanging. In an enchanted castle he encounters wild animals, his bed appears to move, half a body falls down the chimney, he plays nine-pins with human skulls and bones, and much more. But he only learns to fear when his wife – the young queen – one night pours a bucketful of cold water containing gudgeons from the nearby river over him. Gudgeons are just small fish, but they represented his own existential thoughts and they made him shudder. After finally finding them, he was redeemed.

Using the pendulum as applied kinesiology

Kinesiology is an alternative medical treatment, far more comprehensive than can be dealt with in this book. However, one of the central practices of kinesiology is important for what is discussed here: the muscle test. A person holds his or her hand straight (to the front or to the side of the body). A second person pushes on the lower arm for the duration of about a second to move this arm downwards. Normally, it should not be a problem to withstand this type of pressure. However, as soon as a negative stimulus is triggered, the arm can no longer withstand the pressure.

Such negative stimuli may be real objects that make us feel uncomfortable. But they may also be thoughts, words, memories, and ideas of the things we do not like that trigger the negative stimulus and lead to a situation where the arm may be easily pressed down during the muscle test.

Positive and negative thoughts have effect on the muscle tone and muscle tension. The same thing happens with the pendulum.

The Carpenter effect

Experiments within natural science tried to discover what exactly happens when somebody uses a pendulum and called the cause the "ideomotoric law" – the unconscious control of motoric processes.

William Benjamin Carpenter (1813 – 1885), an English scientist, was the first to describe this connection in 1852. The Carpenter effect is a psychological phenomenon wherein the body makes muscular movements independent of conscious desires or emotions.

Newer research (with automatic electroencephalography analysis as well as other methods) has confirmed this psychological law and

has broadened the scope of its application to processes of suggestion, autogenic training, transmittance of facial expression, gestures, and others.

The observation or suggestion (an idea one believes in) of a certain movement triggers a tendency and readiness to *make* these movements. When, we ask a certain question while using the pendulum, in the best of cases our consciousness, which at this moment in time is in a lowered state of consciousness, knows the answer – a solution, a commentary or whatever – to the question posed; and this inner insight triggers a certain movement.

The unconscious forces of dreams, fantasies or visualization practices are the very same forces which influence the movement of the pendulum.

Good vibrations: flowing movements

In terms of the causes for the pendulum's movement, one should be well aware that a pendulum cannot move on its own. It is only the conscious or unconscious movement of a person which makes the pendulum swing. If you fix the pendulum on a post and wait for something to happen, you will wait in vain. Neither the own energy of the pendulum material nor the energy of an object that is brought close to it will trigger any movement (with the exception, of course, of magnets or artificially created electromagnetic fields).

There are several explanations behind why a pendulum swings:

- **Respiratory movements:** Everybody breathes about 16 to 20 times per minute which means the thorax alone is in constant movement. This movement is transmitted down the arm, through the pendulum chain, onto the pendulum itself, and makes it swing.

- **Emotional stimulation:** When we feel joy, fear, sadness or euphoria, this in turn influences our breathing, our pulse, and our blood pressure. This also explains different swings of the pendulum at different times.

- **Unconscious muscle movements:** Unconscious muscle movements: Even when our muscles are completely relaxed they will be active in a degree that we cannot perceive. Even when we think we are holding our hands completely still they will continue to move and these movements are then transmitted onto the pendulum which makes it swing.

- **Unconscious influence:** We all have tiny groups of muscles in our fingertips which cannot be moved consciously. These tiny muscles are the motor of the pendulum. As we cannot make them move by will, this movement is being created unconsciously.

Accepting movement to find rest and peace, being open to answers that originate in stillness, to take decisions and become active – these are the positive effects of working with the pendulum.

Our constant movement is what makes the pendulum swing in the first place, and our conscious as well as our unconscious points of view inform the pendulum's movement; and the result of our work with the pendulum.

These clear explanations help us to understand what happens when we use the pendulum without any superstition. Working with the pendulum is no remedy to all, but it is also not the devil's work, either.

THE PENDULUM AS LANGUAGE OF THE UNCONSCIOUS

Behind all work with the pendulum is the great objective to gain a better understanding of our concerns and needs. We are dealing with the recognition of true longings and the reduction of unnecessary anxieties. This is the opinion of other well-known experts on the pendulum:

"The final authority in each decision needs to be the own 'ego', the inner voice, our gut feeling" (Brigitte Gärtner). "Trust your feelings and emotions – you start to communicate with your subconsciousness and your higher self, the higher wisdom" (Iveta Sloboda).

The unconsciousness of a person contains all that exists – the totality of all that has ever been or may ever come to be, in as far as it has any connection to the person concerned and in as far as he or she hasn't yet noticed it in a conscious way. Even "God", "chance", the cosmos and other spiritual aspects of life belong to the unconsciousness of a person or a society as a whole, as long as they are not in a conscious contact to the matters concerned. Using the pendulum, then, is a possible method to investigate the unconscious in the inner life that actually makes sense. This becomes especially clear when we compare it to two related methods which are also used to get to the bottom of the inner life – the "free association" of Sigmund Freud and the "automatic writing" of André Breton.

Sigmund Freud's "free association"

What was so groundbreaking about this method used by Freud? It was not the famous couch where his patients lay. The couch had been used by others before him, and many of Freud's breakthroughs happened without any involvement of a couch. What was special in relation to Freud's treatment of his patients was that he gave them freedom as long as they kept to the so-called psychoanalytical basic law.

Sigmund Freud (1856 – 1939) required his patients "to refrain from all conscious reflection and to surrender in quiet concentration to the pursuit of their spontaneous [i.e. unwanted] ideas ('they needed to feel the surface of their consciousness')". They were asked to recount these insights and ideas to their therapist "even if they felt exceptions to them, such as that a certain thought was nonsense, or unimportant, or didn't belong here".

Other than the pendulum, Sigmund Freud as a physician at first worked with several methods of "hypnosis" until he decided to work with the interpretation of dreams and free association on the couch. Secondly, Freud stressed that he aimed at the same result with both methods: the inner motivation, the personal concern was taken as the starting point. In both ways, "unconscious material" emerges and this one can learn to interpret.

The use of the pendulum as art

"The Artist's Way" is now a well-known manual and practical guide by Julia Cameron. It offers, as the subtitle states, "A Spiritual Path to Higher Creativity". It contains worthwhile practical advice not only for professional artists, but for all masters of the art of living (this beautiful and effective program will last a few weeks). One basic practice is the daily "morning pages".

Each morning – before you start to do anything else – set aside a few minutes and take some paper, then write down without any conscious agenda and without any direct objective all that comes into your mind. It is important to do this immediately and without any interruption.

This "wild journal writing" is a practice for concentration, relaxation, and decision-making, a playing ground and a motor for creativity which has almost magical implications. Something similar happens when we work with the pendulum and let the pendulum swing above an object or a pendulum table without any conscious agenda or direct aim.

André Breton's "automatic writing"

An artist who discovered and popularized the force of spontaneous writing several decades before Julia Cameron was the French poet, writer and main theoretician of the surrealist movement, André Breton (1896 – 1966). Starting in the early 1920s, he dedicated himself to experiments in hypnotism (which we today would perhaps call "deep meditation") as well as in dream protocols, and he developed "automatic writing".

Automatic writing or *écriture automatique* (today also known as free writing), in its original form, was discovered by the psychologist Pierre Janet. At the end of the 19th century, this pupil of Sigmund Freud suggested the use of this writing process as a method for psychological treatment. The patient, when semisomnolent (either in trance or under hypnosis/deep relaxation) was asked to write to pull the unconscious into his or her consciousness.

André Breton, then, discovered automatic writing in the realm of literature.

When we approach the alphabet of the invisible by consulting the pendulum, we use the force of the frequencies in a similar way to the surrealists. These frequencies do, within us and all around us, express the eternal vitality, the infinite movement of all things living which keeps our lives freshly swinging – and perhaps elevate them to a form of art.

CONSULTING THE PENDULUM WE CONTACT HIGHER FORCES AND THE DEEPER LAYERS OF OUR PERSONALITY. THE INVISIBLE BECOMES VISIBLE.

Basic information about the pendulum

Start immediately

You do not need to know anything to start working with the pendulum. It is like jogging: anyone can do it; you just cannot expect perfect results on your very first jog. It is essentially a method to assist you to bring to light your own emotions, moods, and frequencies and to test them. It also makes it possible for you to experience and understand the higher forces which determine our lives.

When working with the pendulum what is important is that its swing communicates something about your previously unconscious wishes or worries. Therefore, working with the pendulum requires some courage, for a start, the courage to let yourself get involved with your insights and the ideas that will emerge.

Apart from that, there are no secret illusions, no secret language when you consult the pendulum.

Experience and practice make you a master. First of all, get acquainted with a pendulum or even a set of pendulums and experiment with them.

Playfully consulting the pendulum

Among the many oracles available the pendulum is a long-standing method to empty your head in a playful way and to listen to your own heart.

Don't pay heed to any sensationalist story about the discovery of a hidden treasure by a session with a pendulum. Such things might happen – as often as someone wins the lottery.

The real assistance of a pendulum is the way it seems to make the decision for you and in doing that enables you to feel your inner state after this decision. "Only now we may, freed from all inner burden,

notice whether our heart really agrees. Often, the scales fall from our eyes in that very moment. All factual arguments come into mind then as a sudden surprise. Finally, we find an unexpected, but in most cases satisfying solution which pleases reason as well as emotion" (Michael Lemster).

Finding the right pendulum

- To work with the pendulum we need the same combination of deep relaxation and heightened awareness (with complete lack of intention) which we use in all methods of contacting the unconsciousness, be it autogenic training, meditation, the recollection of dreams or consulting the pendulum.
- First drink something which enlivens and refreshes you, be it a cool or a hot drink. Have a wash if you feel the need.
- Warm your hands if you would like to as cold hands may considerably reduce your ability to work with the pendulum.
- It is then important to sit comfortably and upright, with both feet on the ground. Hold your pendulum loosely. Calm your thoughts and be aware of your breathing.
- Imagine in your mind that you have entered a room and leave your worries or excitement behind like a coat in the cloakroom. Here they should remain.
- Breathe deeply. You may move or stretch while doing this. Close your eyes if you feel like doing so. Let your breath go through your whole body, until it reaches your toes, the tips of your hair – and goes beyond that.

Self-assessment

- Tune in internally and practically to your work with the pendulum. Meditate. If urgent wishes or responsibilities cross your mind, note them down or take care of them before you sit down to consult the pendulum.

- Consider whether you are ready for the advice the pendulum will give. Refrain from all advance judgment or expectations.
- Close your eyes and breathe in and out for about a minute. After that with even more quietness and awareness, breathe again, in and out, for a minute. Now the inner contact has been established, and you will feel warmth streaming through your body.
- Switch off and let thoughts come and go.
- Open up. Tell yourself: "Everything is possible when I work with the pendulum." Repeat this sentence several times.
- Be unbiased and open to all possible results.
- Be ready to feel emotionally connected to other people and even other worlds!
- Be honest and loving to yourself and to your neighbor.

PRACTICAL ADVICE

Basic exercise

- Sit down at a table and take the pendulum into your hand. If you are a right-handed person, take the pendulum into your right hand. If you are a left-handed person, take the pendulum into your left hand.
- Take a piece of paper and draw a circle on it. Divide this circle (you may also use a rectangle) into four sections and spontaneously write four of your favorite activities, one in each of the four sections.
- Place the pendulum in the center of the circle or rectangle. Lift your hand so that the pendulum hovers about half an inch above the paper. Remain calm and relaxed and observe what happens and in which direction the pendulum moves most frequently.
- Even experienced practitioners often carry out this exercise. It shows whether you are centered in the present moment, but also what you'd like to do most in a given moment (besides consulting the pendulum).

Mental void and room for something new

You need rest, no distractions and a clear question on your mind (or at least be looking for a clear question), and you need to be prepared to search for an unknown answer in an open and neutral way.

Eliminate annoyances and distractions as far as possible or make them the topic of your question to the pendulum – this way the result will be the more reliable. Concerning the "mental void" as a preparation for openness and a new decisiveness, Roberto Gadini suggests these wonderful exercises:

1ˢᵗ exercise: mental relaxation

Sit down on a comfy chair, put your lower arms on the table and observe the flame of a candle, focusing as much as possible. Do not get distracted by other things which are in the room. After some minutes you will experience a feeling of tension. Pause for a moment, stretch the muscles of your body and only continue with the experiment when you again feel completely relaxed.

If you practice this exercise for about half an hour every day you will soon learn how simple it is to completely detach yourself from your surroundings.

2ⁿᵈ exercise: mental emptiness

If you've practiced the first exercise for a few days, try to do it without using the candle, simply imagine instead. Once you've reached this point try to reduce the candle flame mentally until it has become an infinitely small point of light and, finally, has turned black. Only now have you reached the complete mental void.

Afterwards, imagine the steps of the experiment, and you will create a "conditioned reflex" which enables you to go through the following phases quickly:

1. bodily relaxation,
2. mental relaxation,
3. mental images of the burning flame,
4. image of the point of light,
5. black color,
6. mental emptiness.

When you have practiced this introductory method, continue your training with simple concentration exercises.

Tips and hints

Don't give up too quickly. There will always be distracting factors, but eventually these lose their importance as you progress.

Be aware, for example, of the *jewelry* you wear. It is best to wear no jewelry at all (not even a wristwatch) when you consult the pendulum. It may be possible that your posture is awkward, or that you are being distracted by energies in your immediate surroundings, perhaps the question you've posed makes little sense etc. "Learn by doing!"

Clear all unnecessary objects from the table you are working on; only put those objects on the table with which you want to work, for example the pendulum diagram or the object you want to test with the pendulum.

Don't cross your legs while you sit. When we work with the pendulum, it is a good idea to be earthed, with both feet firmly on the ground in order to allow the energy to flow.

Finally, if a thunderstorm starts, this will often result in distractions which will make using the pendulum impossible.

Which hand should I use?

Experts are divided over that question. Most recommend holding the pendulum in the hand which is used for writing, so that right handed people take the pendulum into their right hand, and left handed people into their left hand. However, to promote the contact with the unconscious, it might be a nice idea to take the hand one does not use for writing.

Often, simple practical exercises will soon indicate which hand can be best used to consult the pendulum. There are no regulations that have to be strictly adhered to. It is also possible to use both hands in turns.

Note: A friend of mine once bowed over a pendulum diagram holding the pendulum chain in her mouth. She wanted to know what it was that she found so difficult to say in this given situation. It worked: The answer of the pendulum made her find the right words.

Holding the pendulums

Usually, the chain of the pendulum will be about 20 cm/8 inches in length. Half of this chain will be held loosely in the hand (from the small finger to the index finger and thumb). The freely swinging part of the chain or thread should measure 10 cm/4 inches. For beginners, it is easier to use a shorter chain. The pendulum should be held in such a way that it may swing unhindered.

2-finger-technique, standard

- Hold the thread or chain firmly, yet relaxed, between thumb and index finger and let the pendulum hang "loosely".
- Your whole hand should be as relaxed as possible.
- Thumb and index finger are in contact to hold the pendulum.
- The aim is to hold the pendulum as freely as possible, that means without putting a hand or an arm on the table. However, beginners may lightly put their arm on a table, which is no problem. Be careful not to angle the wrist joint.
- Thumb and lower arm now form a straight line: this enables the energy to flow freely and thus eases working with the pendulum.

2-finger-technique, palms up

- Take a pendulum whose chain or thread is so long that, if necessary, it may be shortened or stretched.
- Twist the end of the thread or chain around your small finger (or hold to the end with your small finger) so that the rest of the chain or thread does not dangle loosely.
- Hold the thread or chain firmly but relaxed between thumb and index finger and let the pendulum dangle "loosely".
- Now turn your palm upside down and let the thread on which the pendulum hangs glide in the space between thumb and index finger.
- Refrain from propping your arm on the table as this will not allow the pendulum enough space.
- Lightly push your elbow against your body in order to allow your lower arm to rest: in this way, your whole posture is relaxed and receptive.

1-finger-technique, palm up or down

- Take a pendulum whose chain or thread is so long that, if necessary, it may be shortened or stretched.
- Form a relaxed fist and stretch out your index finger (as if you were pointing to something).
- Twist the thread around your index finger once or twice and let the pendulum – there must still be a sufficient length of thread or chain – dangle loosely.
- Twist the end of the thread or chain around your small finger. Take care that you have enough space so you don't hinder the pendulum.
- Now turn your palm upside down so you can see your fingertips. Lightly push your elbow against your body.
- Or: turn your palm down (so you now see your knuckles) and lightly prop your elbow on the table; index finger and lower arm form a straight line, do not angle the wrist joint.

The second hand

In exceptional cases it may assist to work with two pendulums, one in each hand. In normal cases, however, we only use one hand. To advance, consider what to do with your "free" hand (the hand which is not holding the pendulum). Let this hand with palm up rest on the table or in your lap so it cannot affect the swing of the pendulum. Some practitioners put their free hand behind their back to eliminate all possible influence. The posture in which you least tend to think about what to do with your second hand is obviously the best posture!

APPLICATION SPECTRUM

The pendulum can be applied in many different ways. The three most important and popular among this spectrum are:

(1) Using the pendulum with pendulum diagrams
(2) "Mental use of the pendulum"
(3) Using the pendulum to test materials, tolerance etc.

1 Using the pendulum with pendulum diagrams

On the following pages, you will find ready-made as well as blank pendulum diagrams. Carefully read the indications I now give, and you will be able to soon start using the pendulum diagrams.

Indications for pendulum diagrams in form of a circle or rectangle:

In this book you will only find pendulum diagrams with an uneven number of fields. This makes it easier to see into which field the pendulum swings. However, there are also good pendulum diagrams in form of a circle or rectangle with an even number of fields, where the pendulum therefore swings into two opposite fields.

Here, the following rule applies:

First of all take note whether the pendulum swings stronger in one of the opposite fields. If so, the answer is clear.

If the swing of the pendulum is equally strong in both directions (for example to the left and to the right), both answers can be deemed equally valid. If you need to, simply write both answers given on a sheet of paper and use the pendulum separately on this.

You may fashion your own pendulum diagram on any matter you are interested in. Some books offer pendulum diagram with all Bach Flower Essences or with the 144 combinations of oriental and occidental zodiacal signs. But perhaps you are interested in something completely different. Perhaps you use a collection of possible destinations for your

vacation which you note down on a pendulum diagram, or a listing of your former classmates with whom you wish to renew contact. No book can hold all possible pendulum diagrams in store. But you can invent the one that is perfect for you!

2 "Mental use of the pendulum"

Using the pendulum is a path of experience that assists you in making visible your own emotions, frequencies and assumptions, and to test them. It also enables you to experience and fathom the higher forces that determine our lives.

The "mental use of the pendulum" works without pendulum diagrams and without certain objects. We want answers to current questions and to make visible subliminal frequencies in order to recognize them and to act accordingly.

Therefore, we first need to define which swing of the pendulum indicates "yes", "no" or "maybe / don't know". You may keep to existing standards or find your individual code. No matter how you do it – you need to experiment, then experiment, and then experiment again.

"Yes" and "no" – the standards

The commonly used standard definition is that a movement of the pendulum **from the left to the right** indicates **"no"** (as in shaking your head); a movement of the pendulum **back and front** indicates **"yes"** (like nodding). A **circular clockwise movement** means **"yes"**, and a **circular movement against the clock** indicates **"no"**. **Diagonal swings** are taken as meaning **"maybe / don't know"**.

Train and experiment deliberately at first. Tell yourself, tell your inner will in which direction the pendulum should swing: circular to the left or to the right, back and front, or to and fro. Your hand should remain relaxed; the movements of the pendulum should not be visible results of movements of your hand! We do not proceed with force or effort of our will, but with soft force and inner desire.

Practice with a battery

To test your abilities and to train them, here is an exercise taken from Brigitte Gärtner's book "Das Pendel kennt die Antwort" (Munich 1994; www.hkp.ch):

"I am sure there will be a functioning battery somewhere in your household. [...] Put the battery on the table in front of you and take the pendulum in the hand you have resolved to hold it with. Now hold your pendulum above the battery positive terminal (+), and do this so long until the pendulum starts to revolve. Note down the direction in which it revolved. Now hold the pendulum above the battery negative terminal (-) and also note the result.

Repeat this exercise at least ten times and note down your results.

I am not playing a trick on you by asking you to repeat this exercise, because it helps to clear your whole future as a practitioner of the pendulum. At the same time, this exercise assists you in promoting your spontaneous ability as a practitioner and to get used to the pendulum you work with."

Your individual code

Many practitioners only use these standards in exceptional cases. They have found their own "language" in which the pendulum talks to them. They individually define what for them indicates "yes", "no" or "maybe / don't know". Still, even with a personal code you need to definite criteria which must not be changed. You simply choose the pendulum movements to suit your own experience. And this is how it is done:

Ask the pendulum a question where you definitely know the answer – "yes" for example – and observe carefully how the pendulum moves. Take note which movement occurs most often. Here again, the more trials, the more reliable the result will be.

Following the same pattern, take note of the typical movements of your pendulum for "no" or for "maybe".

Draw your personal pendulum movements on a sheet of paper and check them from time to time.

How to proceed practically

- Word your question as carefully as possible.
- Avoid combination questions like: "Shall I do A or B?"
- Choose a question that agrees with your situation or aims.
  It makes quite some difference how you pose a question.
  For example:

**"Shall I do A?" – "What happens when I do A?" – "What can I do
to help make A a success?" – "Where do I find support when I do
A?" – "What opposition do I have to reckon with when I do A?"
– "How will I overcome this opposition?" – etc**

- With many questions, it is helpful to first consider the question
  carefully and then to spontaneously draw up a pendulum
  diagram. For example, focus on the question "Where do I find
  support when I do A?"; then take a sheet of paper and draw a
  circle or rectangle on it. Divide the circle or rectangles into three,
  four or more sectors. Spontaneously note into these sectors all
  possibilities that come to mind – one in each field. If the need
  arises, this exercise can be continued with an additional question
  and more spontaneous pendulum diagrams until you have finally
  reached an answer that satisfies you.
- If you ask questions regarding other people, the pendulum still
  only shows your attitude to the person concerned or to this
  question.
- The pendulum indicates your previously unconscious reactions;
  it is like a mirror into which you look. The way you formulate a
  question will not change this.
- Using the pendulum is a creative process. Don't waste it for
  banalities. Use your creativity for things that are close to your
  heart. Choose your questions accordingly.

3 Using the pendulum to test materials, tolerance etc.

This is a method by which you test whether certain foods are good or bad for you. For doing this, you hold what you want to test in front of you in one hand, and the pendulum in the other between yourself and the object you test.

The answer is given by the pendulum. If it swings back and front, it connects, if it swings from side to side, it pulls apart.

If you do not have the object at hand, you may focus on an image (a photo or a detailed description) or on an object that substitutes the original object.

The use of the pendulum indicates your attitude; it clarifies hints from your unconsciousness. Yet, many questions are not only about attitudes, but also about a practical test. Which medical therapy suits you best, which sport you should take up, what techniques do you like in sex – this and much more you will be able to clear in advance by consulting the pendulum. However, without some real knowledge and a practical test you will not really find an answer.

The pendulum diagrams

Pendulum diagrams for the here and now

Pendulum diagrams for health and well-being

Pendulum diagrams for love and relationships

Pendulum diagrams for business and success

Pendulum diagrams for happiness and contentment

Blank diagrams

(You find a detailed summary on all pendulum diagrams on p. 6)

Here and now:
What shall I do right now?

1 – *Cooking, eating*
2 – *Tidy the room*
3 – *Sports*
4 – *Sleep*
5 – *Work, learn*
6 – *Dance, celebrate*
7 – *Call or visit somebody*
8 – *Something else*
9 – *Continue to use the pendulum*

Here and now:
What shall I do right now?

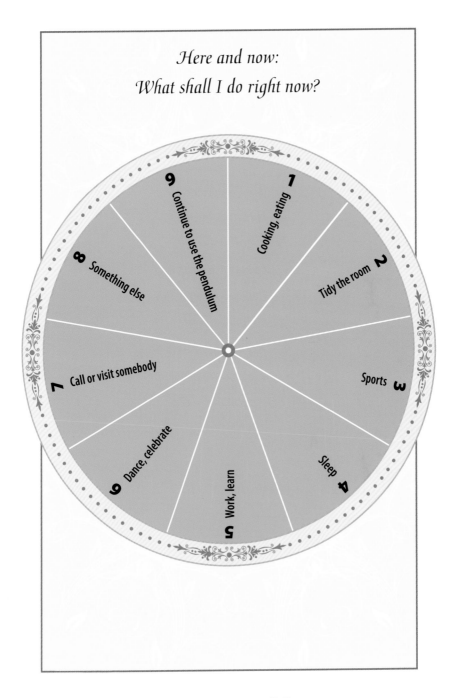

1 Cooking, eating
2 Tidy the room
3 Sports
4 Sleep
5 Work, learn
6 Dance, celebrate
7 Call or visit somebody
8 Something else
9 Continue to use the pendulum

Here and now:
What motivates me right now?

1 – Lust

2 – Trouble, anger

3 – Affection

4 – Disappointment

5 – Happiness, joy

6 – Stress, exhaustion

7 – Hope for recognition

8 – Anticipation, optimism

9 – Envy, impatience

10 – Attention, attentiveness

11 – Something else

Here and now:
What motivates me right now?

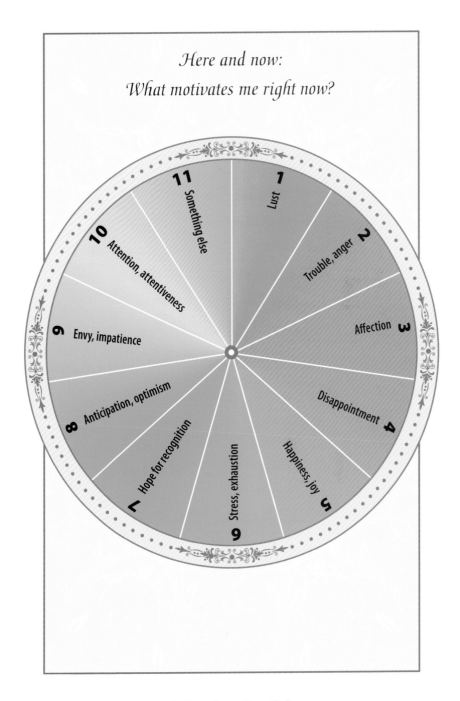

Here and now:
What should I deal with today?

1 – Healthy food
2 – Personal hygiene and body conditioning
3 – Something else
4 – Disease / stress: help others / get help myself
5 – Personal growth and spirituality, new horizons
6 – Training, profession and talent
7 – Friendship and relationships
8 – Relaxation, sport and play
9 – Self-management, setting priorities

Here and now:
What should I deal with today?

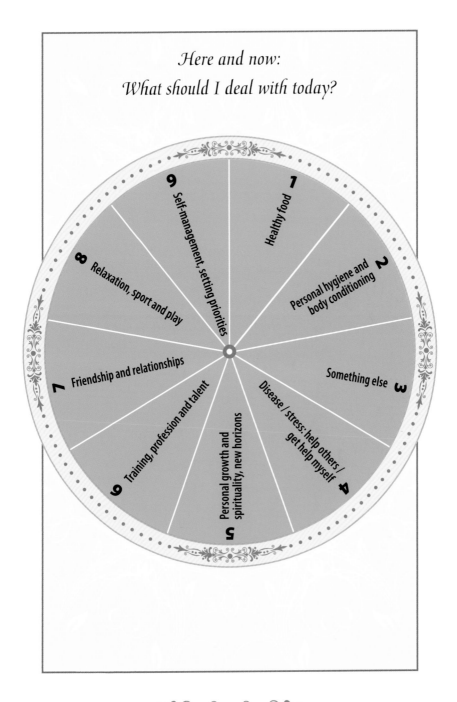

1 Healthy food

2 Personal hygiene and body conditioning

3 Something else

4 Disease / stress: help others / get help myself

5 Personal growth and spirituality, new horizons

6 Training, profession and talent

7 Friendship and relationships

8 Relaxation, sport and play

9 Self-management, setting priorities

Here and now:
Heart-felt wishes, or: what is important now?

1 – Trust someone
2 – Gather new ideas and accept them
3 – Meet an important person
4 – Experience or prepare for a special event
5 – Rethink an old plan
6 – Fulfill a long-held wish
7 – Something else
8 – Just hanging around … and have faith
9 – End a futile project and let it go

Here and now:
Heart-felt wishes, or: what is important now?

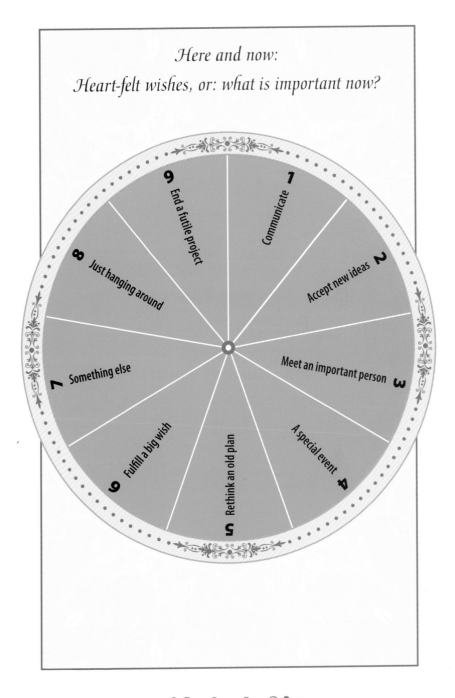

Here and now:
How can I reach my important goals?

1 – *Really want it*

2 – *A personal, 100 per cent effort*

3 – *Get more information*

4 – *Personally take the initiative*

5 – *Something else*

6 – *Sort things, keep them in order*

7 – *See the other side of the coin*

8 – *Planning step-by-step*

9 – *Never give up*

10 – *Forgive myself and others*

11 – *Be consciously aware of "coincidences"*

Here and now:
How can I reach my important goals?

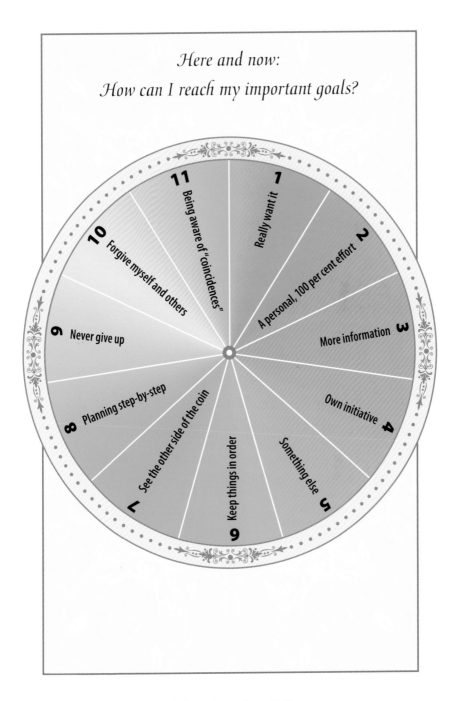

1 Really want it
2 A personal, 100 per cent effort
3 More information
4 Own initiative
5 Something else
6 Keep things in order
7 See the other side of the coin
8 Planning step-by-step
9 Never give up
10 Forgive myself and others
11 Being aware of "coincidences"

Here and now:
What hinders my progress?

1 – *Anything else*

2 – *"I never get the recognition I deserve."*

3 – *"I'll never learn this."*

4 – *"I / we have no chance, anyway."*

5 – *"I'll never manage this on my own."*

6 – *"You can't change the way things are."*

7 – *"Nobody takes me seriously, anyway."*

8 – *"I know everything perfectly."*

9 – *"I'll manage this on my own."*

10 – *"I do know exactly what the others think."*

11 – *"I have everything under control."*

12 – *"I must keep this to myself."*

13 – *"It is my duty."*

14 – *"I don't mind."*

15 – *"I'll never manage this."*

Here and now:
What hinders my progress?

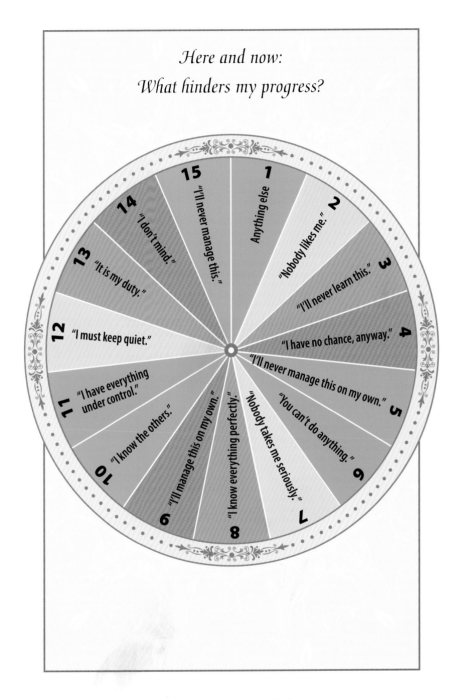

1 Anything else
2 "Nobody likes me."
3 "I'll never learn this."
4 "I have no chance, anyway."
5 "I'll never manage this on my own."
6 "You can't do anything."
7 "Nobody takes me seriously."
8 "I know everything perfectly."
9 "I'll manage this on my own."
10 "I know the others."
11 "I have everything under control."
12 "I must keep quiet."
13 "It is my duty."
14 "I don't mind."
15 "I'll never manage this."

Here and now: Which attitude encourages me,
fosters growth and development?

1 – *"I'll/we'll manage this."*
2 – *"I will get the recognition I deserve."*
3 – *"I'll learn this, we'll learn this."*
4 – *"We still have a chance."*
5 – *"I can do this on my own."*
6 – *"Something can be done about it."*
7 – *Anything else*
8 – *"I remain open and without judgment."*
9 – *"Together we'll manage."*
10 – *"I'll find out what the others want."*
11 – *"Everything is in a flow."*
12 – *"I must not keep this to myself."*
13 – *"I love doing this."*
14 – *"I'll care for this."*
15 – *"I am taken seriously by those in charge."*

Here and now: Which attitude encourages me, fosters growth and development?

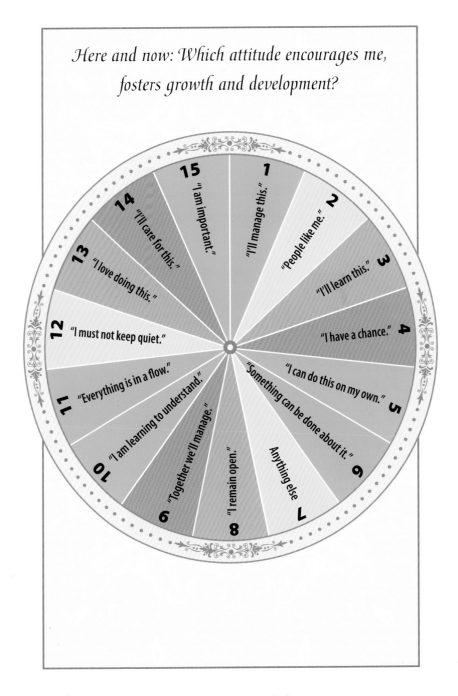

- 1 "I'll manage this."
- 2 "People like me."
- 3 "I'll learn this."
- 4 "I have a chance."
- 5 "Something can be done about it."
- 6 "I can do this on my own."
- 7 Anything else
- 8 "I remain open."
- 9 "Together we'll manage."
- 10 "I am learning to understand."
- 11 "Everything is in a flow."
- 12 "I must not keep quiet."
- 13 "I love doing this."
- 14 "I'll care for this."
- 15 "I am important."

Here and now:
What empowers me and gives me new ideas?

1 – *An atmosphere of gratitude and recognition*
2 – *Fun, humor, entertainment*
3 – *Anything else*
4 – *Meditation, rest, loneliness*
5 – *Giving and receiving signs of love*
6 – *Sex and eroticism*
7 – *Journeys and travelling*
8 – *Sleeping and dreaming*
9 – *My friends*
10 – *My family*
11 – *Being surrounded by nature*

Here and now:
What empowers me and gives me new ideas?

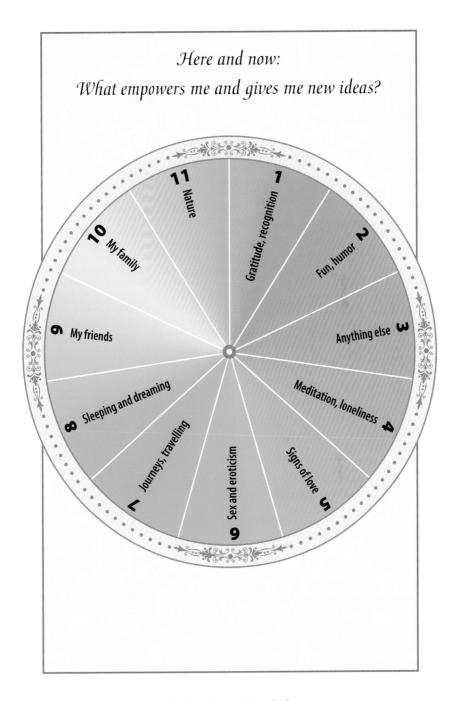

Here and now:
What talent can I now develop?

1 – Enthusiastic
2 – Playful
3 – Strong
4 – Insistent
5 – Genuine, authentic
6 – Reflective
7 – Practical, realistic
8 – Courageous
9 – Curious
10 – Willing to learn
11 – Imaginative
12 – Generous
13 – Beautiful
14 – Strong-willed
15 – Sexy
16 – Something else
17 – Reasonable
18 – Full of lust / fun
19 – Compassionate
20 – Passionate
21 – Informed, communicative
22 – Affectionate, friendly
23 – Sensual, down-to-earth
24 – Trustful, open
25 – Careful

Here and now:
What talent can I now develop?

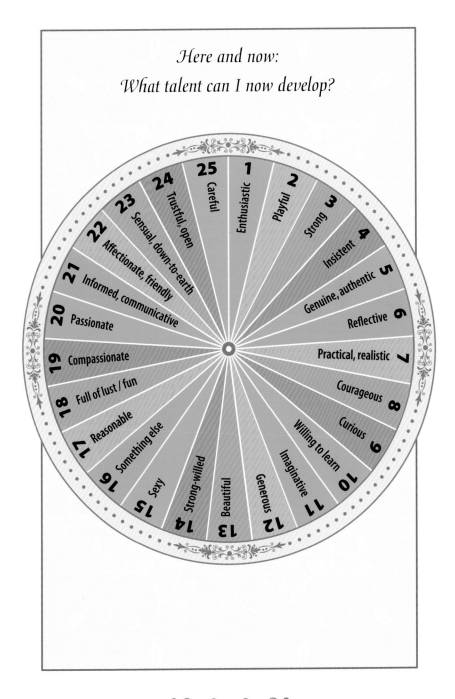

Here and now: From which of my energy centers do I get most power now?

1 – 1st Chakra (Root Chakra)
2 – 2nd Chakra (Sacral Chakra)
3 – 3rd Chakra (Solar Plexus Chakra)
4 – 4th Chakra (Heart Chakra)
5 – 5th Chakra (Throat Chakra)
6 – 6th Chakra (Third Eye Chakra)
7 – 7th Chakra (Crown Chakra)
8 – Whole person
9 – Choose different question

Here and now: From which of my energy centers do I get most power now?

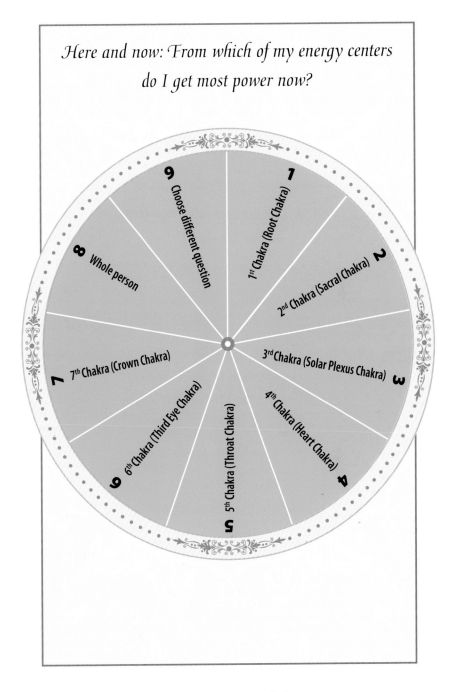

9 Choose different question

1 1st Chakra (Root Chakra)

8 Whole person

2 2nd Chakra (Sacral Chakra)

7 7th Chakra (Crown Chakra)

3 3rd Chakra (Solar Plexus Chakra)

6 6th Chakra (Third Eye Chakra)

4 4th Chakra (Heart Chakra)

5 5th Chakra (Throat Chakra)

Health and well-being:
My Health

1 – I feel good.

2 – I feel bad.

3 – I need to go see a doctor.

4 – I don't care right now.

5 – Something is wrong, but it is nothing medical.

6 – I have known worse times.

7 – I care for myself.

8 – I'll get advice.

9 – I have trust in the future.

10 – I have regular medical check-ups.

11 – I get information from reliable sources.

Health and well-being:
My Health

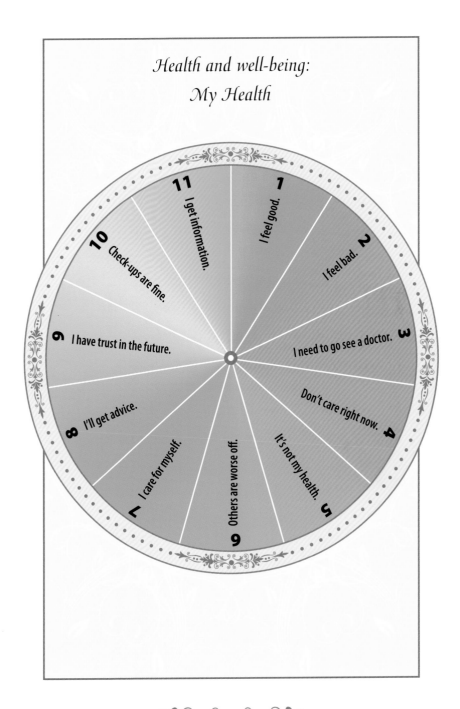

- 1 I feel good.
- 2 I feel bad.
- 3 I need to go see a doctor.
- 4 Don't care right now.
- 5 It's not my health.
- 6 Others are worse off.
- 7 I care for myself.
- 8 I'll get advice.
- 9 I have trust in the future.
- 10 Check-ups are fine.
- 11 I get information.

Health and well-being:
My key to well-being

1 – Personal hygiene
2 – Care for the soul
3 – Self-esteem
4 – Friendship, recognition
5 – Relationship, love
6 – Work, task
7 – Success, money, reputation
8 – Profession, calling
9 – Art, design
10 – Nature, naturalness
11 – Adventure
12 – Something else / ask differently
13 – Humor, laughter
14 – Family, children, (chosen) relatives
15 – Soul searching

Health and well-being:
My key to well-being

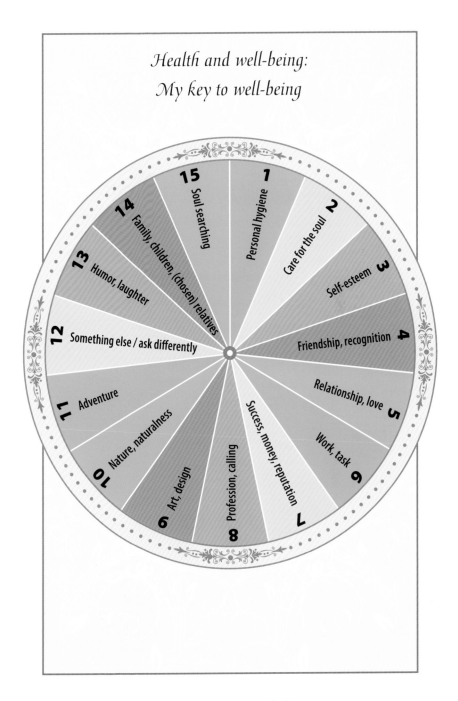

Health and well-being:
My sexuality

1 – *Not important at the moment.*

2 – *I can't think of anything else.*

3 – *Why don't I do it?*

4 – *Love is giving me wings.*

5 – *I have desires that I need to care about now.*

6 – *I have feelings of guilt I need to clear now.*

7 – *Each morning, the sun rises anew.*

8 – *Opportunity makes us love.*

9 – *All is possible, nothing is a must.*

10 – *Without love no lust.*

11 – *Ask a different question.*

Health and well-being:
My sexuality

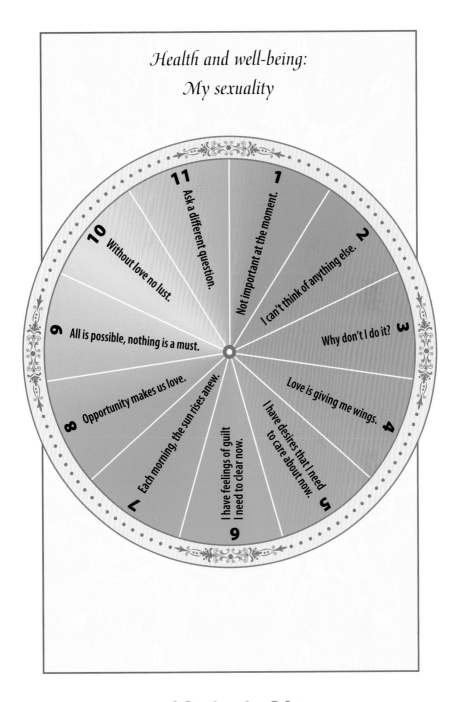

1 — Not important at the moment.
2 — I can't think of anything else.
3 — Why don't I do it?
4 — Love is giving me wings.
5 — I have desires that I need to care about now.
6 — I have feelings of guilt I need to clear now.
7 — Each morning, the sun rises anew.
8 — Opportunity makes us love.
9 — All is possible, nothing is a must.
10 — Without love no lust.
11 — Ask a different question.

Health and well-being:
Which food is really good for me?

1 – Berries, wild berries
2 – Citrus fruits
3 – Meat
4 – Green salads, vegetables
5 – Fish, shellfish
6 – Soy products
7 – Rice and cereal products
8 – Mixed salad, mixed vegetable
9 – Milk, dairy products
10 – Sprout, cabbage, broccoli
11 – Eggs
12 – Nuts
13 – Potatoes, pumpkins, bananas
14 – Leguminous plants
15 – Leafy vegetables (spinach etc.)
16 – Fruit vegetables (tomatoes etc.)
17 – Carrots
18 – Hot vegetables, spices
19 – Mushrooms
20 – Apples, cherries
21 – Apricots, peaches
22 – Cooking oil
23 – Something else / different question
24 – Chocolate, cocoa
25 – Other fruits

Health and well-being: Which food is really good for me?

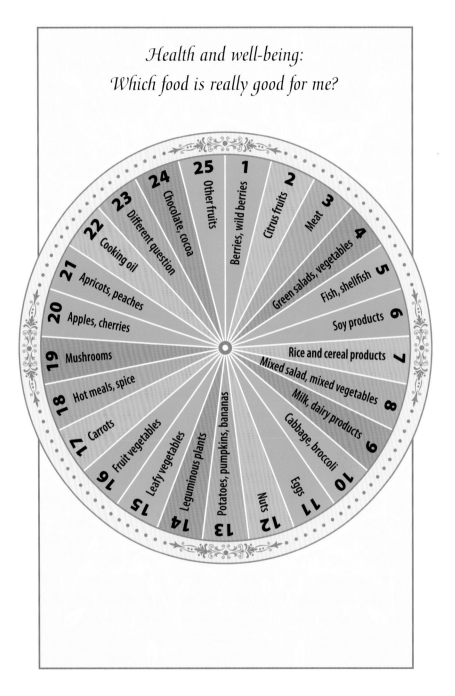

- 1 Berries, wild berries
- 2 Citrus fruits
- 3 Meat
- 4 Green salads, vegetables
- 5 Fish, shellfish
- 6 Soy products
- 7 Rice and cereal products
- 8 Mixed salad, mixed vegetables
- 9 Milk, dairy products
- 10 Cabbage, broccoli
- 11 Eggs
- 12 Nuts
- 13 Potatoes, pumpkins, bananas
- 14 Leguminous plants
- 15 Leafy vegetables
- 16 Fruit vegetables
- 17 Carrots
- 18 Hot meals, spice
- 19 Mushrooms
- 20 Apples, cherries
- 21 Apricots, peaches
- 22 Cooking oil
- 23 Different question
- 24 Chocolate, cocoa
- 25 Other fruits

Health and well-being:
which foods should I avoid right now?

1 – Berries, wild berries
2 – Citrus fruits
3 – Meat
4 – Green salads, vegetables
5 – Fish, shellfish
6 – Soy products
7 – Rice and cereal products
8 – Mixed salad, mixed vegetable
9 – Milk, dairy products
10 – Sprout, cabbage, broccoli
11 – Eggs
12 – Nuts
13 – Potatoes, pumpkins, bananas
14 – Leguminous plants
15 – Leafy vegetables (spinach etc.)
16 – Fruit vegetables (tomatoes etc.)
17 – Carrots
18 – Hot vegetables, spices
19 – Mushrooms
20 – Apples, cherries
21 – Apricots, peaches
22 – Cooking oil
23 – Something else / different question
24 – Chocolate, cocoa
25 – Other fruits

Health and well-being:
which foods should I avoid right now?

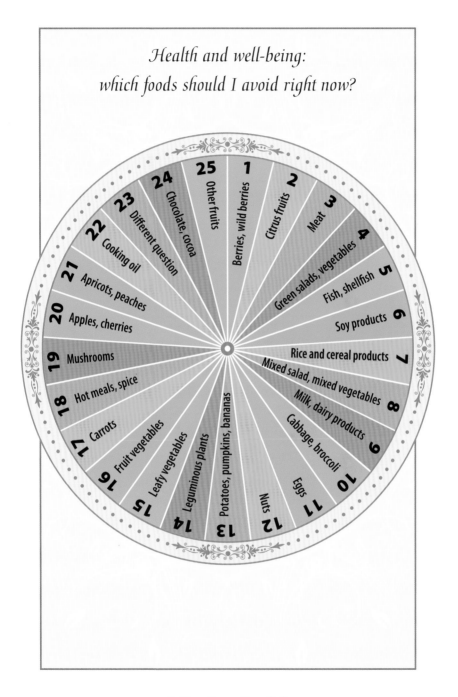

1 Berries, wild berries
2 Citrus fruits
3 Meat
4 Green salads, vegetables
5 Fish, shellfish
6 Soy products
7 Rice and cereal products
8 Mixed salad, mixed vegetables
9 Milk, dairy products
10 Cabbage, broccoli
11 Eggs
12 Nuts
13 Potatoes, pumpkins, bananas
14 Leguminous plants
15 Leafy vegetables
16 Fruit vegetables
17 Carrots
18 Hot meals, spice
19 Mushrooms
20 Apples, cherries
21 Apricots, peaches
22 Cooking oil
23 Different question
24 Chocolate, cocoa
25 Other fruits

Health and well-being:
What helps with my allergy / my ill-defined pain?

1 – Kneippism / increasing my resistance
2 – More sleep
3 – More sex
4 – Enjoy a sauna
5 – See a doctor
6 – Eat no animal protein
7 – Eat no dairy products
8 – Eat no animal fat
9 – More sweets
10 – Less sweets
11 – Less or no alcohol
12 – Less acid
13 – More sports
14 – Massage, physiotherapy
15 – Being in the open air
16 – Express emotions
17 – Handle emotions, meditation
18 – Psychotherapy, counseling
19 – Food without preservatives
20 – Food without industrial sugar
21 – Food without yeast and artificial ingredients
22 – Something else / different question
23 – More assertiveness, more success
24 – Forgiveness, more trust in God, letting go
25 – Take over a task, responsibility

Health and well-being:
What helps with my allergy / my ill-defined pain?

1. Kneippism / increasing my resistance
2. More sleep
3. More sex
4. Enjoy a sauna
5. See a doctor
6. Eat no animal protein
7. Eat no dairy products
8. Eat no animal fat
9. More sweets
10. Less sweets
11. Less or no alcohol
12. Less acid
13. More sports
14. Massage, physiotherapy
15. Being in the open air
16. Express emotions
17. Handle emotions, meditation
18. Psychotherapy, counseling
19. No preservatives
20. No industrial sugar
21. No yeast or artificial ingredients
22. Something else / different question
23. Assertiveness, success
24. Forgiveness, letting go
25. Task, responsibility

71

Health and well-being:
What kind of personal hygiene should I enjoy now?

1 – Haircut, head massage

2 – Cosmetic treatment, counseling

3 – Skin care

4 – Facial care, make-up, facial massage

5 – Other massage

6 – Facial pack

7 – Physiotherapy, gymnastics

8 – Manicure, pedicure

9 – Mouth and dental care

10 – Something else

11 – Sun bath, hot air, color or light shower

12 – Dark room, eye mask, fresh air, coolness

13 – Sweating

14 – Rest, lazing around

15 – Bath, hydrotherapy

Health and well-being:
What kind of personal hygiene should I enjoy now?

1. Haircut, head massage
2. Cosmetic treatment, counseling
3. Skin care
4. Facial care, make-up, facial massage
5. Other massage
6. Facial pack
7. Physiotherapy, gymnastics
8. Manicure, pedicure
9. Mouth and dental care
10. Something else
11. Sun bath, light shower
12. Dark room, coolness
13. Sweating
14. Rest, lazing around
15. Bath, hydrotherapy

Health and well-being: Which part of my body should I especially love and care for?

1 – Immune system, balance (of the soul)
2 – Heart, circulation
3 – Respiration
4 – Bladder and urinary tract
5 – Glands
6 – Skeleton, bones
7 – Joints
8 – Nerves
9 – Skin
10 – Hair and nails
11 – Sexual organs
12 – Digestive organs
13 – Spinal column and cervical vertebra
14 – Muscles and sinews
15 – Connective tissue and cartilage
16 – Something else / different question
17 – Seeing, recognize
18 – Feeling, touch
19 – Smell, instinct
20 – Taste, refine
21 – Hearing, differentiate
22 – Teeth, bite
23 – Endurance
24 – Metabolism, basal energy rate
25 – Flexibility, movement

Health and well-being: Which part of my body should I especially love and care for?

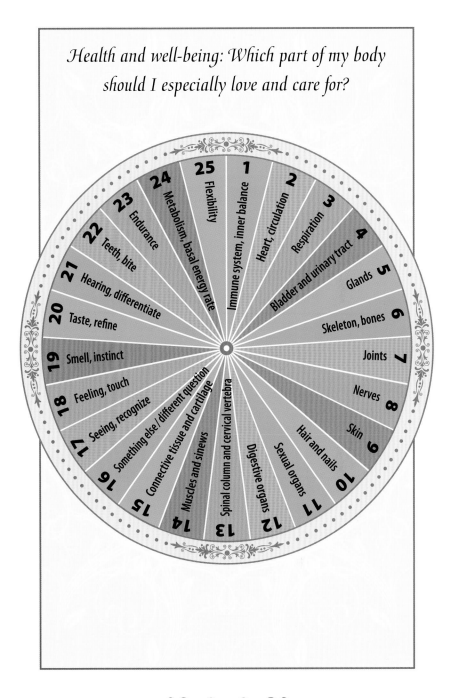

Immune system, inner balance — 1
Heart, circulation — 2
Respiration — 3
Bladder and urinary tract — 4
Glands — 5
Skeleton, bones — 6
Joints — 7
Nerves — 8
Skin — 9
Hair and nails — 10
Sexual organs — 11
Digestive organs — 12
Spinal column and cervical vertebra — 13
Muscles and sinews — 14
Connective tissue and cartilage — 15
Something else / different question — 16
Seeing, recognize — 17
Feeling, touch — 18
Smell, instinct — 19
Taste, refine — 20
Hearing, differentiate — 21
Teeth, bite — 22
Endurance — 23
Metabolism, basal energy rate — 24
Flexibility — 25

Health and well-being:
Which conventional therapy should I try?

1 – Psychotherapy

2 – Confession, spiritual guidance, prayer

3 – Discussion group, self-help group

4 – Art therapy, painting therapy

5 – New hobby

6 – Care for an animal

7 – Speech therapy / rhetorical counseling, self-expression

8 – "Retreat" (time off for contemplation)

9 – "Religious exercises" (spiritual exercises),
stay in a monastery

10 – "Fast", days of fasting

11 – Kneippism

12 – Schroth treatment

13 – Sleep treatment

14 – Drinking treatment

15 – Other treatment

16 – Hiking, pilgrimage

17 – Vacation

18 – Stay by the sea

19 – Stay in the mountains

Health and well-being:
Which conventional therapy should I try?

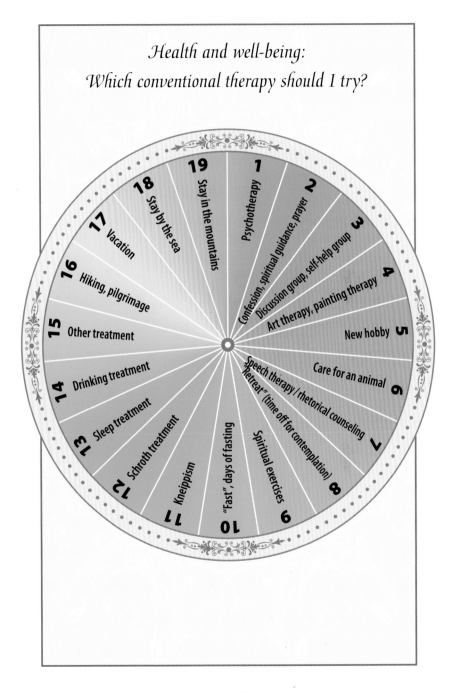

1. Psychotherapy
2. Confession, spiritual guidance, prayer
3. Discussion group, self-help group
4. Art therapy, painting therapy
5. New hobby
6. Care for an animal
7. Speech therapy / rhetorical counseling
8. "Retreat" (time off for contemplation)
9. Spiritual exercises
10. "Fast", days of fasting
11. Kneippism
12. Schroth treatment
13. Sleep treatment
14. Drinking treatment
15. Other treatment
16. Hiking, pilgrimage
17. Vacation
18. Stay by the sea
19. Stay in the mountains

Health and well-being:
Which alternative therapy should I try?

1 – Homeopathy
2 – Acupuncture, TCM
3 – Shiatsu
4 – Yoga
5 – Taj Chi, Qi Gong
6 – Karate, Kung Fu, Ju-do u. a.
7 – Chakra work
8 – Meditation, silence
9 – Tantra
10 – Drumming
11 – Shamanic rituals, sweat hut
12 – Naturopathy treatment
13 – Vegetarian diet
14 – Uncooked vegetarian food
15 – Ayurvedic diet and treatment
16 – Reiki, energy work, quantum healing
17 – Light therapy, color therapy
18 – Sound therapy, sound massage, musical therapy
19 – Primal scream, intuitive and spiritual singing
20 – Samadhi-Tank, dark room
21 – Cryotherapy, cold temperature room
22 – Dream work, hypnotic therapy
23 – Aromatherapy, essences
24 – Herbal remedies
25 – Dietary supplement

Health and well-being:
Which alternative therapy should I try?

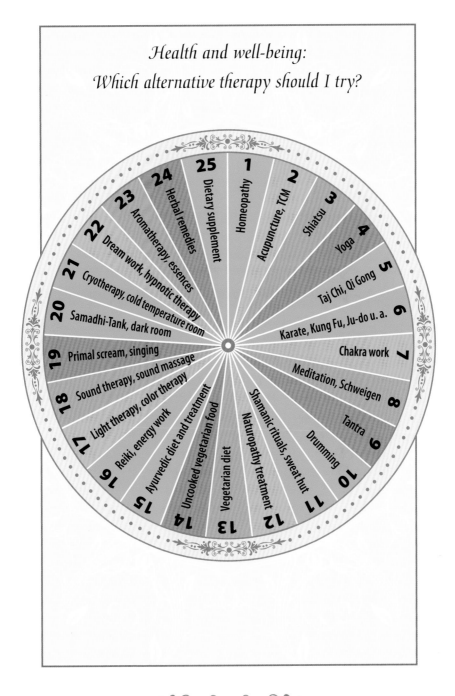

1 Homeopathy
2 Acupuncture, TCM
3 Shiatsu
4 Yoga
5 Taj Chi, Qi Gong
6 Karate, Kung Fu, Ju-do u. a.
7 Chakra work
8 Meditation, Schweigen
9 Tantra
10 Drumming
11 Shamanic rituals, sweat hut
12 Naturopathy treatment
13 Vegetarian diet
14 Uncooked vegetarian food
15 Ayurvedic diet and treatment
16 Reiki, energy work
17 Light therapy, color therapy
18 Sound therapy, sound massage
19 Primal scream, singing
20 Samadhi-Tank, dark room
21 Cryotherapy, cold temperature room
22 Dream work, hypnotic therapy
23 Aromatherapy, essences
24 Herbal remedies
25 Dietary supplement

Love and relationships: Current situation of my relationship / search for a partner

1 – *Everything is fine!*

2 – *I am irritated.*

3 – *Setting clear limits is good.*

4 – *I want to know it precisely.*

5 – *Other*

6 – *I can forgive.*

7 – *I don't need to be perfect / don't need to apologize.*

8 – *I live life a little less ordinary.*

9 – *Time is on our side.*

Love and relationships: Current situation of my relationship / search for a partner

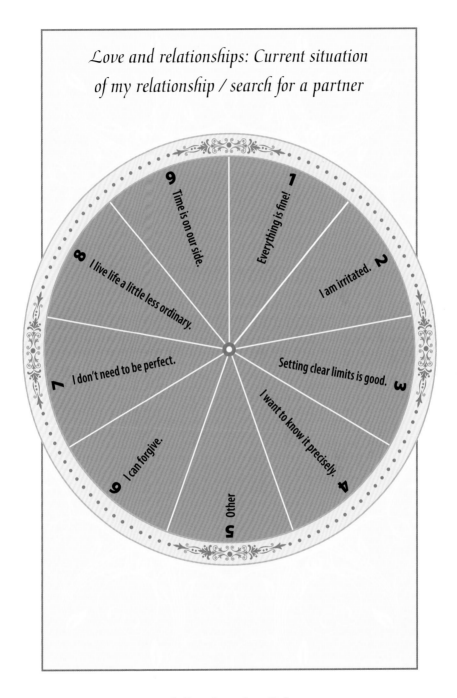

- 1 Everything is fine!
- 2 I am irritated.
- 3 Setting clear limits is good.
- 4 I want to know it precisely.
- 5 Other
- 6 I can forgive.
- 7 I don't need to be perfect.
- 8 I live life a little less ordinary.
- 9 Time is on our side.

Love and relationships:
My family (apartment-sharing community etc.)

1 – Together, we experience more.

2 – Other

3 – I need to communicate something.

4 – A joy shared is a joy doubled.

5 – A problem shared is a problem halved.

6 – We are a fantastic team.

7 – I'd prefer more appreciation.

8 – There is no need to understand everything.

9 – I care for myself, which is enough.

10 – Time for a change of scene

11 – I've had enough!

Love and relationships:
My family (apartment-sharing community etc.)

1 Together, we experience more.

2 Other

3 I need to communicate something.

4 A joy shared is a joy doubled.

5 A problem shared is a problem halved.

6 We are a fantastic team.

7 I'd prefer more appreciation.

8 There is no need to understand everything.

9 I care for myself, which is enough.

10 Time for a change of scene

11 I've had enough!

Love and relationships:
Gifts of love are goodies – what to do now

1 – *Listen*
2 – *Give presents*
3 – *Have confidence*
4 – *Be critical*
5 – *Give praise*
6 – *Other*
7 – *Help, ask*
8 – *Wait*
9 – *Silence*

Love and relationships:
Gifts of love are goodies – what to do now

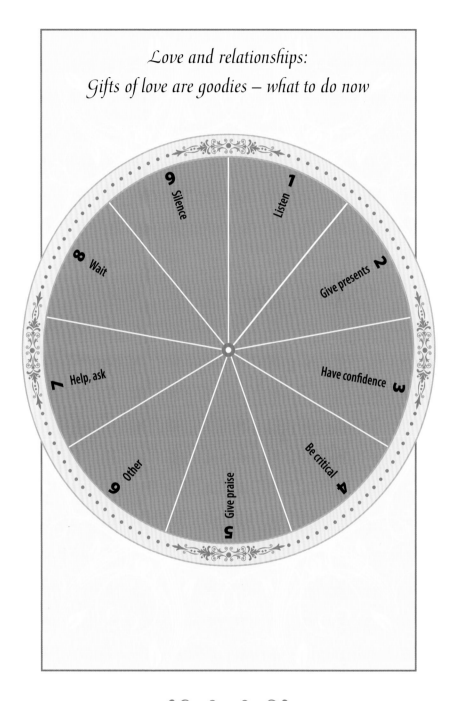

1 Listen
2 Give presents
3 Have confidence
4 Be critical
5 Give praise
6 Other
7 Help, ask
8 Wait
9 Silence

Love and relationships:
Current state of my love life

1 – I am happy.

2 – I am bored.

3 – He / she loves me.

4 – He / she doesn't love me.

5 – I need time to think.

6 – I don't want to wait any longer.

7 – I say "no".

8 – I say "yes".

9 – I need more distance.

10 – We could spend more time together.

11 – I don't know, I am confused.

Love and relationships:
Current state of my love life

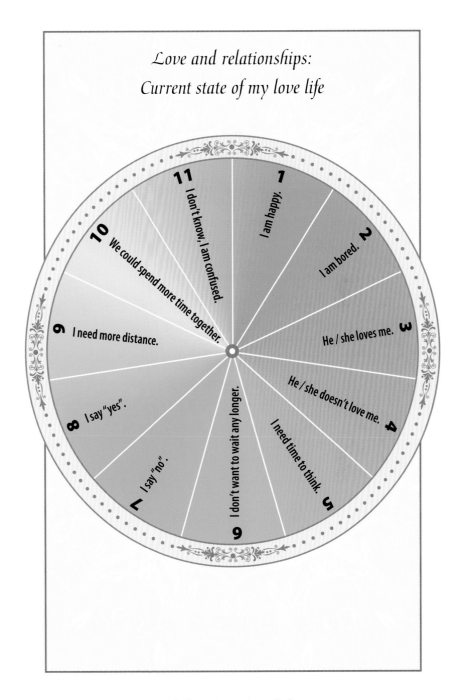

1 I am happy.

2 I am bored.

3 He / she loves me.

4 He / she doesn't love me.

5 I need time to think.

9 I don't want to wait any longer.

7 I say "no".

8 I say "yes".

9 I need more distance.

10 We could spend more time together.

11 I don't know, I am confused.

Love and relationships:
My aims in love

1 – *Travel together*
2 – *Work together*
3 – *Joint household*
4 – *Own family*
5 – *Discussion*
6 – *Request for forgiveness*
7 – *No envy*
8 – *I need some variety*
9 – *More rest*
10 – *Better conversation*
11 – *Better sex*
12 – *Other*
13 – *Joint project*
14 – *Separate bedrooms*
15 – *More independence*

Love and relationships:
My aims in love

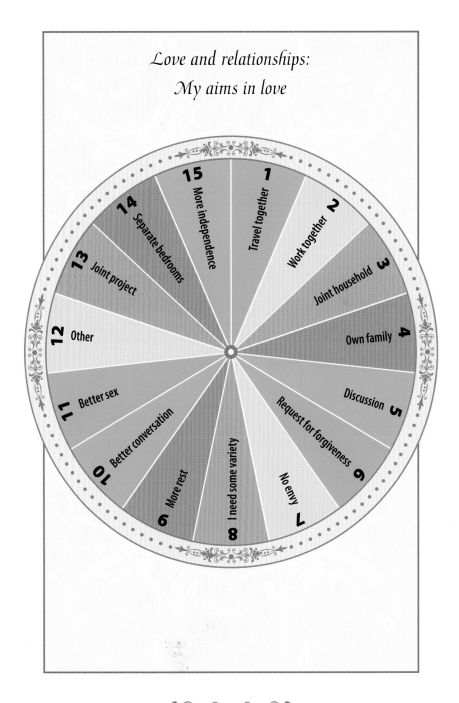

The wheel contains the following numbered aims:

1. Travel together
2. Work together
3. Joint household
4. Own family
5. Discussion
6. Request for forgiveness
7. No envy
8. I need some variety
9. More rest
10. Better conversation
11. Better sex
12. Other
13. Joint project
14. Separate bedrooms
15. More independence

Love and relationships: Love is just a word – or: what keeps us together?

1 – Romance and tenderness

2 – Shared free time

3 – Sex and eroticism

4 – Similar hobbies

5 – Other

6 – Similar attitudes and ideas

7 – Habits

8 – Shared passions, aims and tasks

9 – Stress and quarreling

10 – Gratitude

11 – Enjoying being together

12 – Curiosity, love of experimenting

13 – Fear of separation

14 – (Vague) hope

15 – Shared work

Love and relationships: Love is just a word – or: what keeps us together?

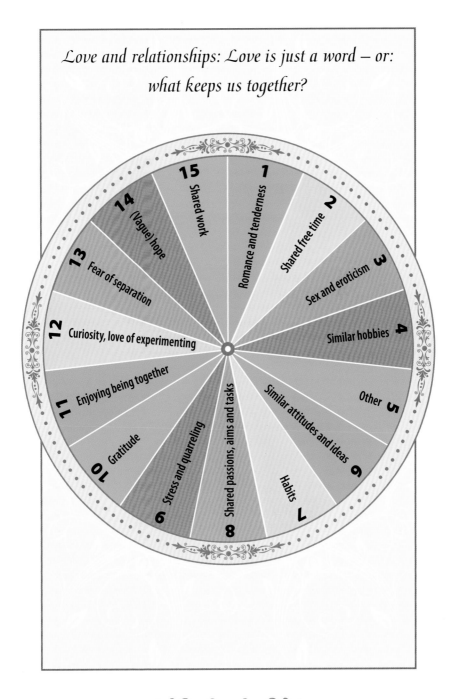

- 1 Romance and tenderness
- 2 Shared free time
- 3 Sex and eroticism
- 4 Similar hobbies
- 5 Other
- 6 Stress and quarreling
- 7 Habits
- 8 Shared passions, aims and tasks
- 9 Similar attitudes and ideas
- 10 Gratitude
- 11 Enjoying being together
- 12 Curiosity, love of experimenting
- 13 Fear of separation
- 14 (Vague) hope
- 15 Shared work

Love and relationships: What will benefit your relationship or search for a partner?

1 – *Self-love, complacency*
2 – *Sexual experiments and erotic adventure*
3 – *Peace and positive routine*
4 – *Meditation, being happy alone*
5 – *Going on holidays together*
6 – *Something else*
7 – *Patience and endurance*
8 – *Taking the initiative*
9 – *Asserting clear demands*
10 – *Letting go of all demands or preconditions*
11 – *Talking about things*
12 – *Keeping something to yourself*
13 – *Stressing your female qualities*
14 – *Stressing your male qualities*
15 – *Going on holidays alone*

Love and relationships: What will benefit your relationship or search for a partner?

1 Self-love, complacency

2 Sexual experiments and erotic adventure

3 Peace and positive routine

4 Meditation, being happy alone

5 Going on holidays together

6 Something else

7 Patience and endurance

8 Taking the initiative

6 Asserting clear demands

10 Letting go of all demands or preconditions

11 Talking about things

12 Keeping something to yourself

13 Stressing your female qualities

14 Stressing your male qualities

15 Going on holidays alone

Love and relationships: Which erotic fantasy would you like to fulfil now?

1 – Tender words

2 – Tender touch

3 – Wild words

4 – Wild touch

5 – Disguises, games

6 – Stripping, revelations

7 – Sexual experiments

8 – Sexual balance

9 – Declaration of love (to someone)

10 – Declaration of love (to yourself)

11 – Something else

Love and relationships: Which erotic fantasy would you like to fulfil now?

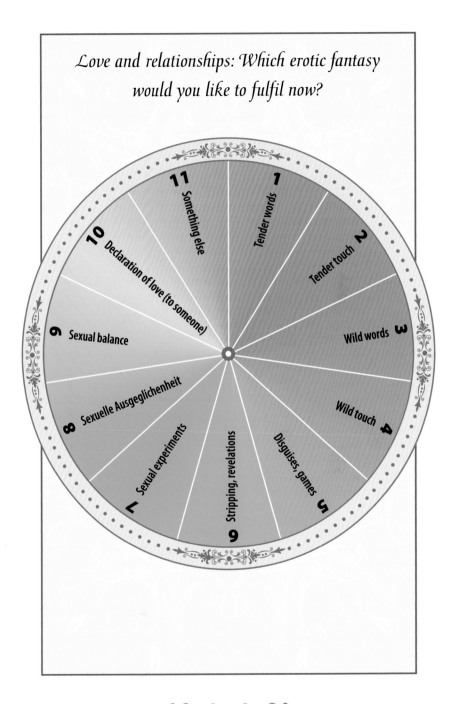

- 1 Tender words
- 2 Tender touch
- 3 Wild words
- 4 Wild touch
- 5 Disguises, games
- 9 Stripping, revelations
- 7 Sexual experiments
- 8 Sexuelle Ausgeglichenheit
- 9 Sexual balance
- 10 Declaration of love (to someone)
- 11 Something else

Love and relationships:
Inspiring natural resources for love*

1 – *Sage*
2 – *Sandal-wood*
3 – *(Bitter-) Orange*
4 – *Spruce, spruce needle*
5 – *Jasmine*
6 – *Peppermint*
7 – *Lemon grass*
8 – *Cinnamon*
9 – *Lavender*
10 – *Something else*
11 – *Original cacao*
12 – *Roses*
13 – *Valerian*
14 – *Verbena*
15 – *Apple*
16 – *Violet*
17 – *Tomatoes*
18 – *Carrots*
19 – *Ginger*
20 – *Strawberries*
21 – *Elder*
22 – *Hawthorn*
23 – *Vanilla*
24 – *Ylang-Ylang*
25 – *Thyme*

Love and relationships:
Inspiring natural resources for love*

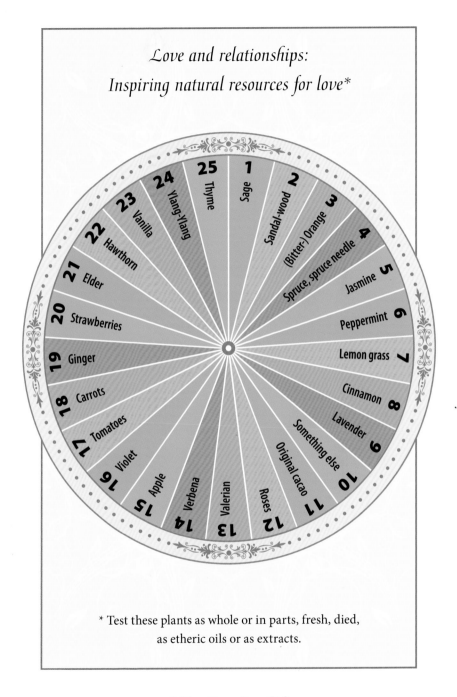

* Test these plants as whole or in parts, fresh, died,
as etheric oils or as extracts.

Love and relationships: Valuable experiences which give you a new strength to love

1 – Happy moments of childhood

2 – Special experiences in childhood

3 – Happy moments of adulthood

4 – Special experiences in the middle of life

5 – Happy moments of old age

6 – A particular birthday

7 – Particular moments of being in love

8 – A test passed

9 – A disease healed

10 – A threat overcome

11 – A problem solved

12 – A special success

13 – A certain declaration of love

14 – Special moments of happiness

15 – A moment of great gratitude

Love and relationships: Valuable experiences which give you a new strength to love

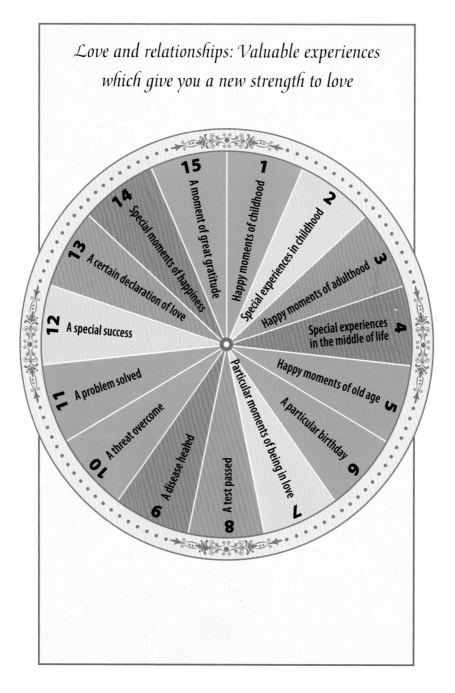

1. Happy moments of childhood
2. Special experiences in childhood
3. Happy moments of adulthood
4. Special experiences in the middle of life
5. Happy moments of old age
6. A particular birthday
7. Particular moments of being in love
8. A test passed
9. A disease healed
10. A threat overcome
11. A problem solved
12. A special success
13. A certain declaration of love
14. Special moments of happiness
15. A moment of great gratitude

Profession and success:
My situation at work …

1 – *Work is my life.*
2 – *I love what I am doing.*
3 – *Everything is O.K.*
4 – *I'll fight for this project.*
5 – *I hate what I am doing.*
6 – *Only the outcome counts.*
7 – *It is time for a pay rise.*
8 – *I'll fight for my rights.*
9 – *I support others.*

Profession and success:
My situation at work …

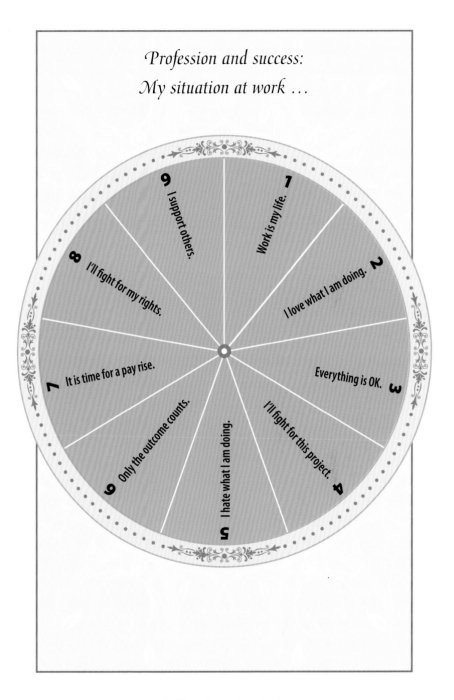

Profession and success:
What about my performance?

1 – I am satisfied.

2 – I am stuck at the moment.

3 – Too much work.

4 – Too little work.

5 – I need to test the results.

6 – The results are O.K.

7 – I need to test the prerequisites / objectives.

8 – Other

9 – New ideas are needed.

10 – New partners are required.

11 – Prerequisites / objectives are O.K.

Profession and success:
What about my performance?

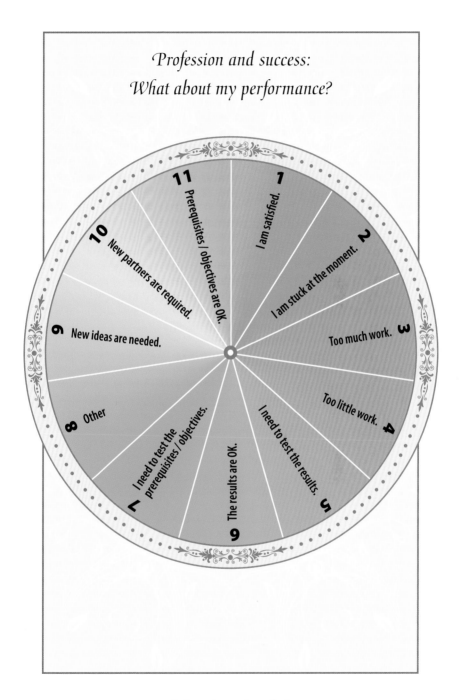

Profession and success:
My current objectives for success

1 – More money

2 – More time

3 – More joy and passion

4 – More recognition and praise

5 – Going freelance

6 – Other

7 – Rehabilitate old values

8 – Contribute more

9 – Withdrawal

10 – Bequeath something, empower others

11 – New values, establish new rules

Profession and success:
My current objectives for success

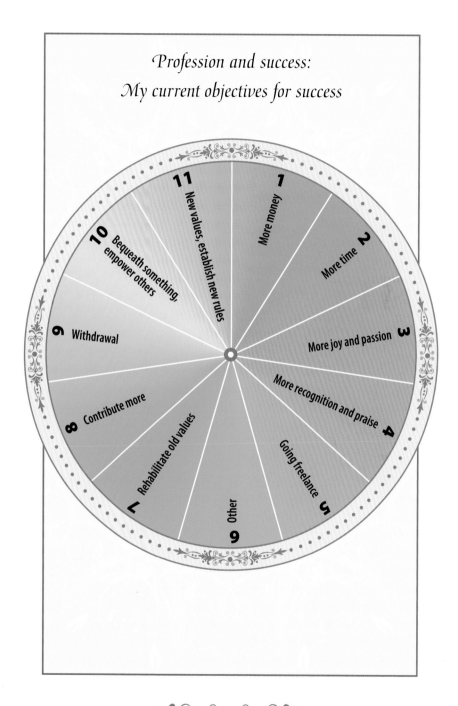

- 11 New values; establish new rules
- 1 More money
- 10 Bequeath something, empower others
- 2 More time
- 9 Withdrawal
- 3 More joy and passion
- 4 More recognition and praise
- 8 Contribute more
- 7 Rehabilitate old values
- 5 Going freelance
- 9 Other

Profession and success:
Which attitude empowers me?

1 – "There is nothing good – unless you do it (yourself)."

2 – "I am unique – but not well-behaved!"

3 – "There is nothing that can disfigure a beautiful woman or man."

4 – "Some like me – all others, go away!"

5 – "I can do without everything – but luxury."

6 – "I love myself, and I don't mind whom I marry (so why not my profession?)."

7 – "You need so little to be happy ..."

8 – "The art of living is the highest art."

9 – "There is always a possibility."

Profession and success:
Which attitude empowers me?

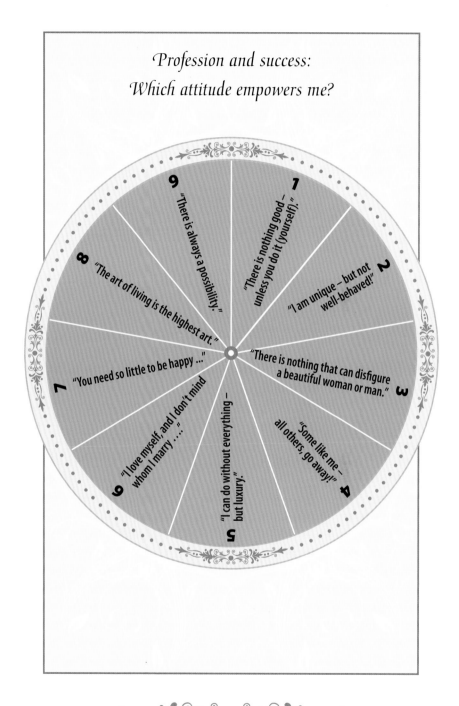

9 "There is always a possibility."

1 "There is nothing good – unless you do it (yourself)."

8 "The art of living is the highest art."

2 "I am unique – but not well-behaved!"

"You need so little to be happy …"

"There is nothing that can disfigure a beautiful woman or man." 3

7

"I love myself, and I don't mind whom I marry …"

"Some like me – all others, go away!" 4

6

"I can do without everything – but luxury."

5

Profession and success:
The right moment

1 – *Today*

2 – *Always now*

3 – *Tomorrow*

4 – *In a week*

5 – *In 10 days*

6 – *In two weeks*

7 – *In a month*

8 – *Ask anew and differently*

9 – *In 100 days*

Profession and success:
The right moment

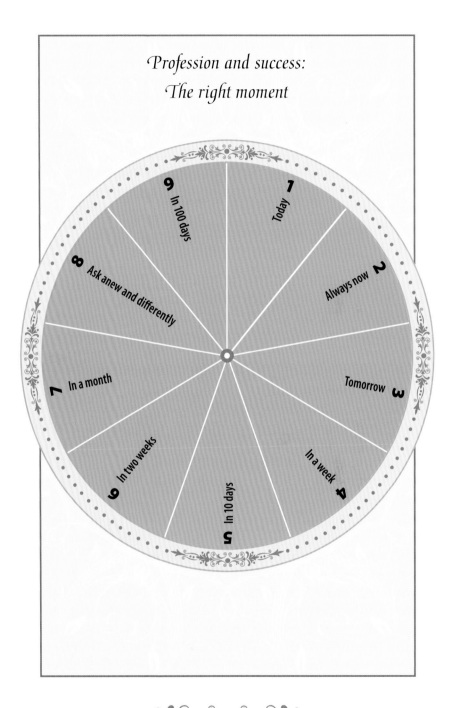

Profession and success:
What is best for me right now?

1 – *Inspiration: oracle and meditation*

2 – *Transpiration: "learning" and working hard"*

3 – *Enthusiasm, enthuse others*

4 – *Something completely different*

5 – *Courage to criticize and reflect*

6 – *Strength for humility and modesty*

7 – *Anger that helps overcome obstacles*

8 – *Endurance*

9 – *Lists and tricks*

10 – *Faith and trust*

11 – *Ask the experts*

12 – *Disproving of experts*

13 – *Keeping to the rules*

14 – *Bypassing of the rules*

15 – *Learning, learning …*

Profession and success:
What is best for me right now?

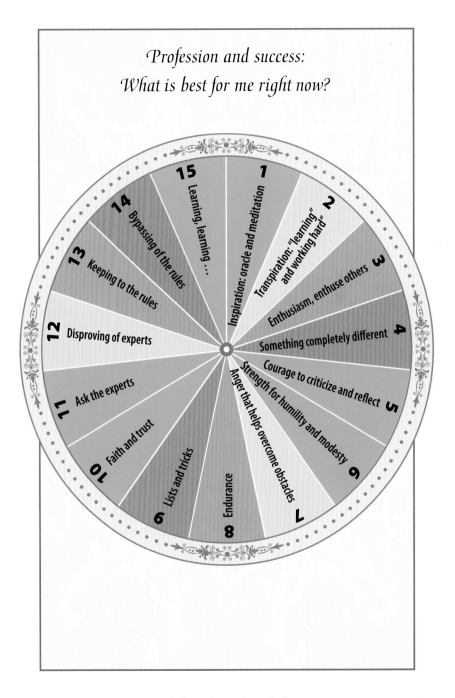

Inspiration: oracle and meditation
1

Transpiration: "learning" and working hard"
2

Enthusiasm, enthuse others
3

Something completely different
4

Courage to criticize and reflect
Strength for humility and modesty
5

Anger that helps overcome obstacles
7

Endurance
8

9

Lists and tricks
6

Faith and trust
10

Ask the experts
11

Disproving of experts
12

Keeping to the rules
13

Bypassing of the rules
14

Learning, learning …
15

Profession and success:
Which profession suits me best?

1 – *Art, design*
2 – *School, education*
3 – *Craft*
4 – *Fitness, wellness*
5 – *Office work*
6 – *Caring for the aged*
7 – *Technology, other*
8 – *Agriculture*
9 – *Sylviculture*
10 – *Administration*
11 – *Banking*
12 – *(Tele-) communication*
13 – *Culture, events management*
14 – *Consumer protection, consumer advice*
15 – *Social services*
16 – *Management and organization*
17 – *Electronics and IT*
18 – *Promotion, marketing*
19 – *Medical professions*
20 – *Care, nursing for the sick, healing*
21 – *Something else*
22 – *Hotel and catering industry*
23 – *Media and journalism*
24 – *Engineer*
25 – *Sports*

Profession and success:
Which profession suits me best?

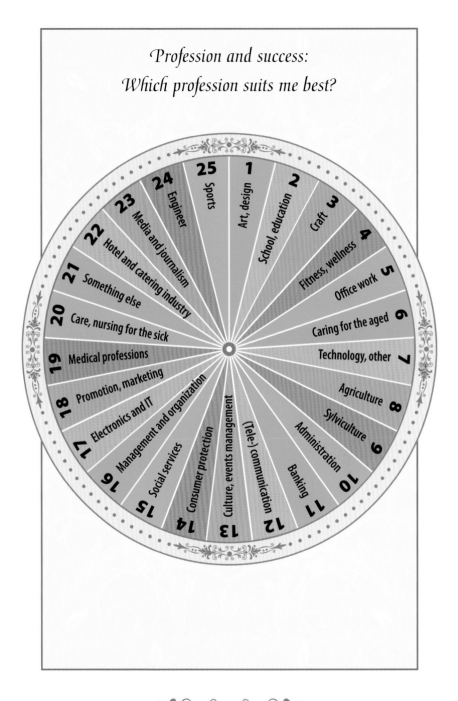

1. Art, design
2. School, education
3. Craft
4. Fitness, wellness
5. Office work
6. Caring for the aged
7. Technology, other
8. Agriculture
9. Sylviculture
10. Administration
11. Banking
12. (Tele-) communication
13. Culture, events management
14. Consumer protection
15. Social services
16. Management and organization
17. Electronics and IT
18. Promotion, marketing
19. Medical professions
20. Care, nursing for the sick
21. Something else
22. Hotel and catering industry
23. Media and journalism
24. Engineer
25. Sports

Profession and success:
What training would help me most right now?

1 – Management training
2 – Presentation techniques
3 – Book keeping
4 – Body training
5 – Etiquette, lifestyle training
6 – Articulation lessons
7 – Training to sing
8 – Something else
9 – Dance training, dancing lessons
10 – Massage training
11 – Learning to cook
12 – Learning languages
13 – Computer training
14 – Qualifying examination
15 – University studies

Profession and success:
What training would help me most right now?

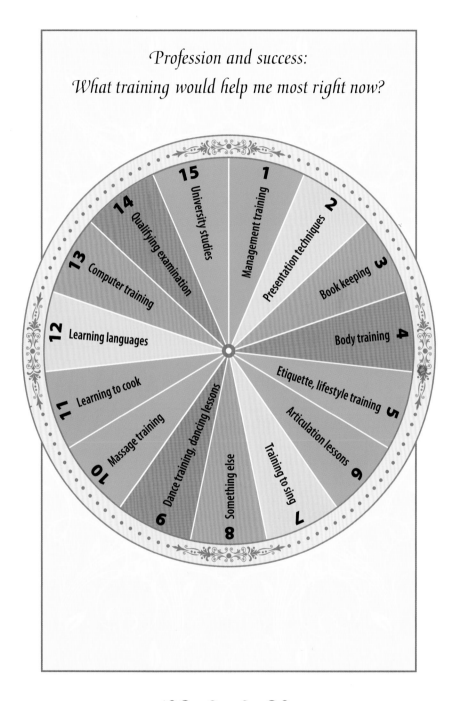

1 Management training
2 Presentation techniques
3 Book keeping
4 Body training
5 Etiquette, lifestyle training
6 Dance training, dancing lessons
7 Training to sing
8 Something else
9 Articulation lessons
10 Massage training
11 Learning to cook
12 Learning languages
13 Computer training
14 Qualifying examination
15 University studies

Profession and success: What should I pay special attention to in my work right now?

1 – Organization

2 – Business model, business plan

3 – Something else / different question

4 – Preparation and planning

5 – Efficiency, rationalization

6 – Clear perspectives for all

7 – Potential for growth

8 – Research and development

9 – Cost accounting, controlling

10 – Conflict management

11 – Control, evaluation

12 – Profit, secure profits

13 – Profile of the enterprise, marketing

14 – Communication, branch, internet

15 – Team spirit, joint activities

Profession and success: What should I pay special attention to in my work right now?

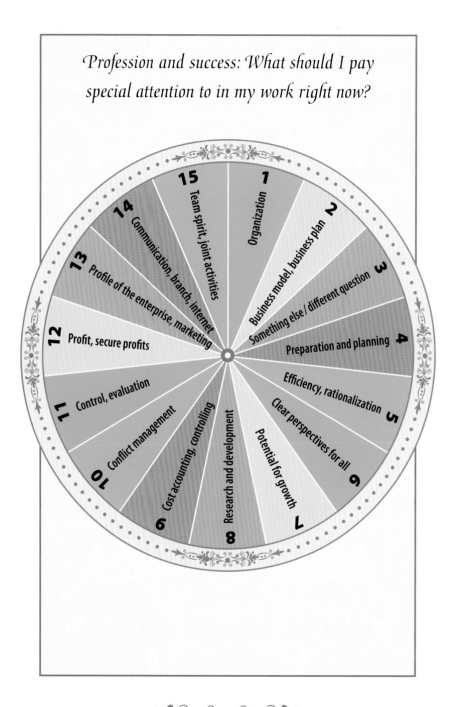

Profession and success: The secret of my success – what I can learn from others

1 – Aries: impulsive, energetic, self-governing – "I am."

2 – Taurus: enduring, practical, sensual – "I have."

3 – Gemini: fast as lightning, erratic, communicative – "I think."

4 – Cancer: headstrong, emotional, skeptical – "I feel."

5 – Leo: courageous, robust, vain – "I want."

6 – Virgo: self-secure, cool, regulative – "I differentiate / analyze."

7 – Libra: harmonic, creative, harsh – "I balance."

8 – Scorpio: intensive, jealous, focused – "I demand."

9 – Sagittarius: enthusiastic, quick, idealistic – "I see, I proclaim."

10 – Capricorn: ambitious, faithful, striving – "I use."

11 – Aquarius: strong in will, independent, friendly – "I know."

12 – Pisces: sensitive, subtle, dreamy – "I believe."

13 – Totality of the strength of all zodiacal signs

14 – Something else / different question

15 – I am my very own zodiacal sign.

Profession and success: The secret of my success – what I can learn from others

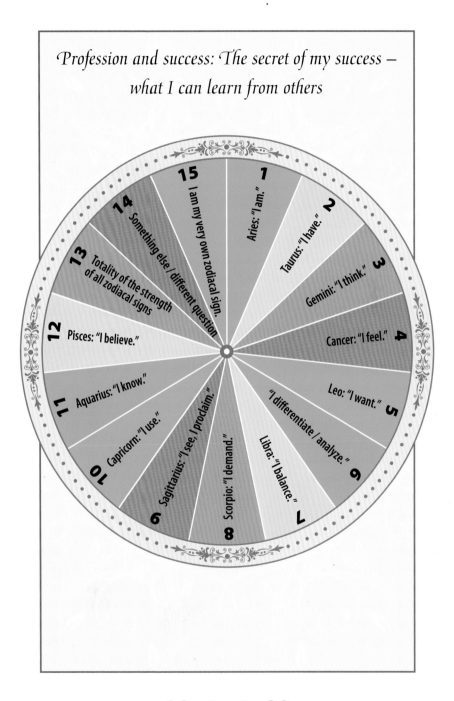

1 – Aries: "I am."
2 – Taurus: "I have."
3 – Gemini: "I think."
4 – Cancer: "I feel."
5 – Leo: "I want."
6 – "I differentiate / analyze."
7 – Libra: "I balance."
8 – Scorpio: "I demand."
9 – Sagittarius: "I see, I proclaim."
10 – Capricorn: "I use."
11 – Aquarius: "I know."
12 – Pisces: "I believe."
13 – Totality of the strength of all zodiacal signs
14 – Something else / different question
15 – I am my very own zodiacal sign.

Happiness and contentment:
What about my happiness?

1 – *Everything is fine.*

2 – *Something is missing.*

3 – *Something else.*

4 – *It's better than I had thought.*

5 – *Important wishes have been fulfilled.*

6 – *Important wishes are still open.*

7 – *Problems need to be solved.*

8 – *We are working on the problems.*

9 – *Have patience!*

Happiness and contentment: What about my happiness?

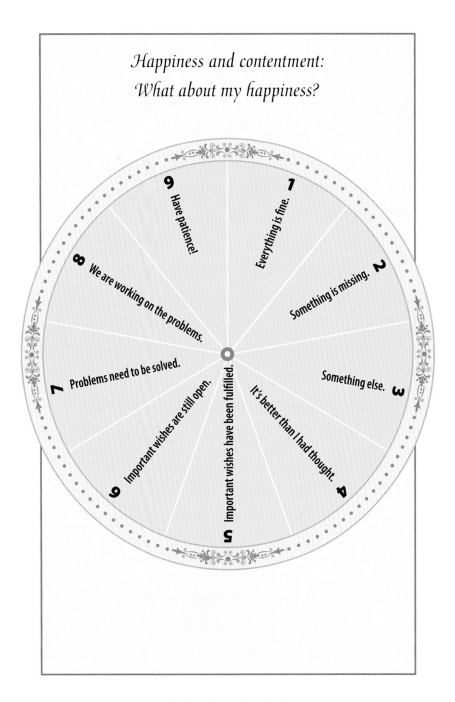

- 1 Everything is fine.
- 2 Something is missing.
- 3 Something else.
- 4 It's better than I had thought.
- 5 Important wishes have been fulfilled.
- 6 Important wishes are still open.
- 7 Problems need to be solved.
- 8 We are working on the problems.
- 9 Have patience!

Happiness and contentment:
My concept of happiness – my current objectives

1 – *Study, teach*

2 – *Work with a purpose, honorary post*

3 – *Celebrate*

4 – *Help, works of love*

5 – *Pamper myself*

6 – *Pamper partner, friends*

7 – *Time with the family*

8 – *Time on my own*

9 – *Lust, eroticism*

10 – *Sports, games, dance*

11 – *Foreign languages, travelling*

12 – *Painting, creating*

13 – *Writing, telling*

14 – *Music, movies, photos*

15 – *Construct, handicraft work*

16 – *Nature, garden*

17 – *House and home*

18 – *Religion, spirituality*

19 – *Idling*

Happiness and contentment:
My concept of happiness – my current objectives

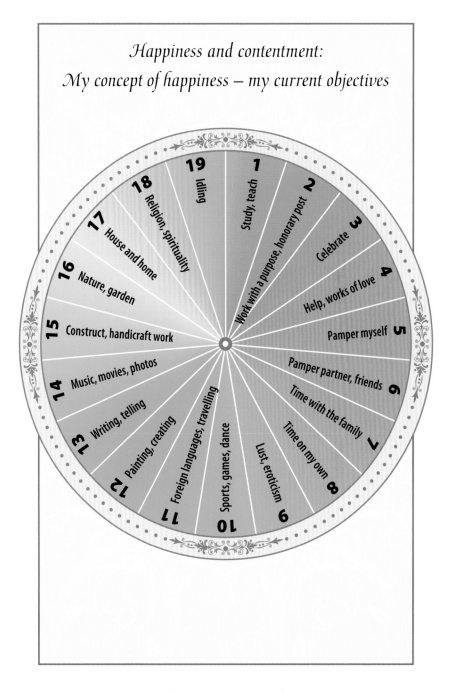

The diagram is a wheel with the following segments:

1. Study, teach
2. Work with a purpose, honorary post
3. Celebrate
4. Help, works of love
5. Pamper myself
6. Pamper partner, friends
7. Time with the family
8. Time on my own
9. Lust, eroticism
10. Sports, games, dance
11. Foreign languages, travelling
12. Painting, creating
13. Writing, telling
14. Music, movies, photos
15. Construct, handicraft work
16. Nature, garden
17. House and home
18. Religion, spirituality
19. Idling

Happiness and contentment:
Time for a change …

1 – *I will follow up "coincidences".*
2 – *Something else / different question*
3 – *I will clear old stuff out from my home.*
4 – *A spontaneous holiday is the thing to do.*
5 – *I will write a love letter.*
6 – *An argument will be closed.*
7 – *I will pay my debts.*
8 – *I will ask for what I deserve.*
9 – *Let's tackle unfinished business.*

Happiness and contentment:
Time for a change …

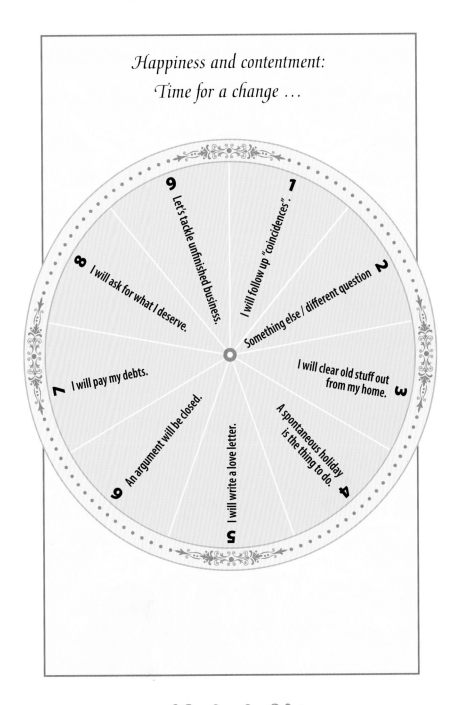

1. I will follow up "coincidences".
2. Something else / different question
3. I will clear old stuff out from my home.
4. A spontaneous holiday is the thing to do.
5. I will write a love letter.
6. An argument will be closed.
7. I will pay my debts.
8. I will ask for what I deserve.
9. Let's tackle unfinished business.

Happiness and contentment:
My next vacation …

1 – *Soon*

2 – *Later*

3 – *At home*

4 – *By the seaside*

5 – *In the mountains*

6 – *In the countryside*

7 – *In a metropolis*

8 – *On my own*

9 – *Something else*

10 – *To unknown shores*

11 – *A pilgrimage*

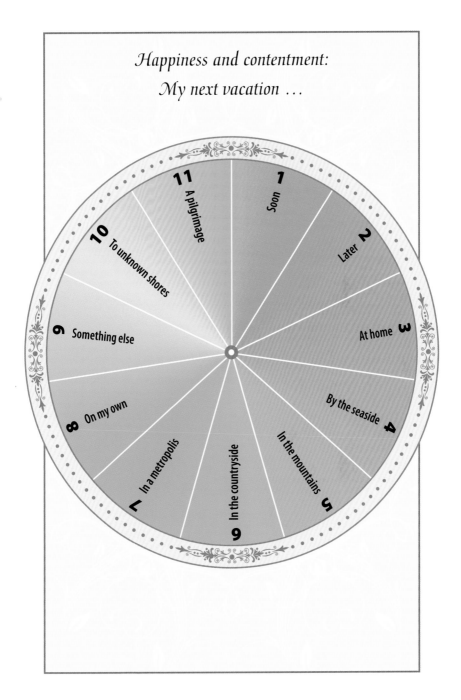

Happiness and contentment:
My next vacation …

Happiness and contentment:
What will make me happy now?

1 – Participate more
2 – Enter a new friendship or relationship
3 – Laugh again
4 – Cry
5 – Be content and happy
6 – Make others happy
7 – Something else / different question
8 – Get healthy, stay healthy
9 – Recover from shock
10 – Be productive, be creative
11 – Be flexible, have strength
12 – Start new adventures
13 – Get some rest
14 – Be authentic, less " false compromise"
15 – Say goodbye
16 – Keep a distance
17 – Have patience
18 – Express anger or use it creatively
19 – Forgive again and again

Happiness and contentment:
What will make me happy now?

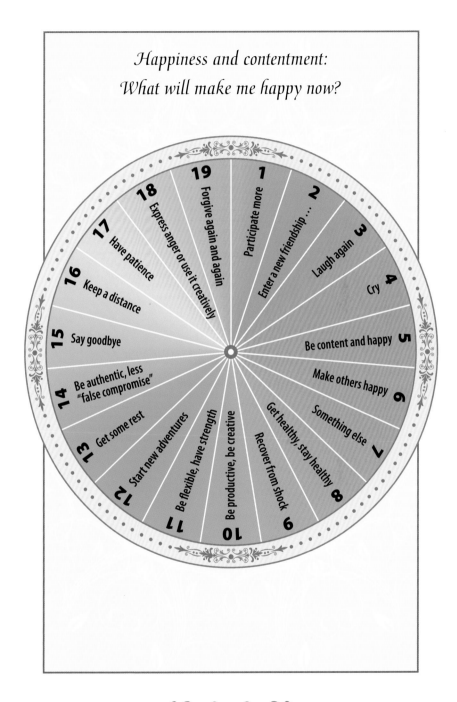

1. Participate more
2. Enter a new friendship . . .
3. Laugh again
4. Cry
5. Be content and happy
6. Make others happy
7. Something else
8. Get healthy, stay healthy
9. Recover from shock
10. Be productive, be creative
11. Be flexible, have strength
12. Start new adventures
13. Get some rest
14. Be authentic, less "false compromise"
15. Say goodbye
16. Keep a distance
17. Have patience
18. Express anger or use it creatively
19. Forgive again and again

Happiness and contentment:
What should I change now in the way I live?

1 – *More sleep and rest at night*

2 – *More relaxation*

3 – *More exercise*

4 – *More fresh air*

5 – *Eat healthier*

6 – *Allow yourself to have no plan, follow your "gut feeling"*

7 – *Something else / different question*

8 – *Less extremes*

9 – *Do all that is important more slowly*

10 – *Finish all that is important*

11 – *Admit more reason and realism*

Happiness and contentment:
What should I change now in the way I live?

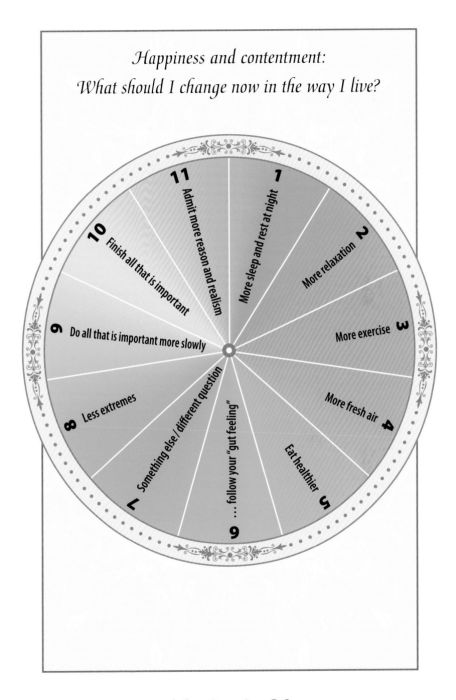

- 11 — Admit more reason and realism
- 1 — More sleep and rest at night
- 2 — More relaxation
- 3 — More exercise
- 4 — More fresh air
- 5 — Eat healthier
- 9 — ...follow your "gut feeling"
- 7 — Something else / different question
- 8 — Less extremes
- 9 — Do all that is important more slowly
- 10 — Finish all that is important

Happiness and contentment:
My best way to relax

1 – Lying on the couch, content
2 – Listen to music, make music
3 – Sports
4 – Solve a problem
5 – Have fun with others
6 – Go for a long walk
7 – Pamper my pet
8 – Give myself a present
9 – Cook a good meal
10 – Do something
11 – Gardening
12 – Take a trip
13 – Eat in a fine restaurant
14 – Book a journey
15 – Help a friend

Happiness and contentment:
My best way to relax

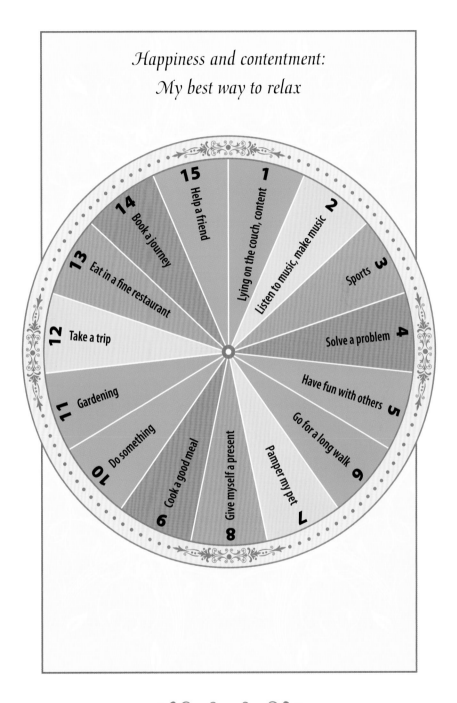

1 Lying on the couch, content
2 Listen to music, make music
3 Sports
4 Solve a problem
5 Have fun with others
6 Go for a long walk
7 Pamper my pet
8 Give myself a present
9 Cook a good meal
10 Do something
11 Gardening
12 Take a trip
13 Eat in a fine restaurant
14 Book a journey
15 Help a friend

Happiness and contentment:
My best way to high spirits

1 – *Something else / different question*
2 – *Do something useful, get things done*
3 – *Call someone or write a letter*
4 – *Switch off with a book or film*
5 – *Wash, bathe, swim*
6 – *Music, dance*
7 – *Movies, theater*
8 – *Do nothing*
9 – *Socialise*

Happiness and contentment:
My best way to high spirits

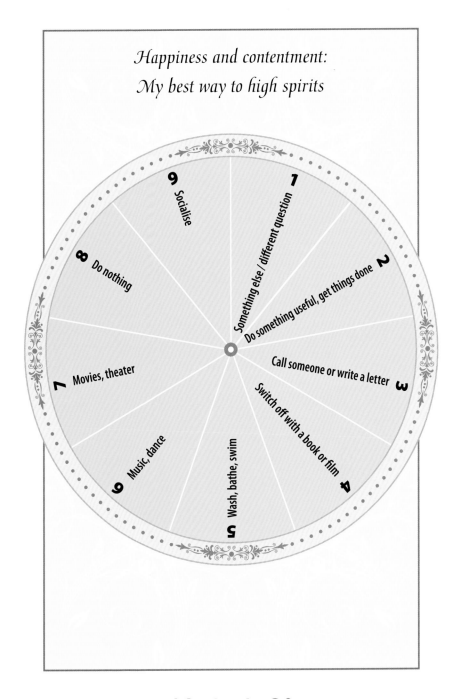

1 — Something else / different question
2 — Do something useful, get things done
3 — Call someone or write a letter
4 — Switch off with a book or film
5 — Wash, bathe, swim
6 — Music, dance
7 — Movies, theater
8 — Do nothing
9 — Socialise

Happiness and contentment:
Which oracle best supports my current intuition?

1 – *Tarot cards*

2 – *I Ging*

3 – *Runes*

4 – *Numerology*

5 – *Astrology*

6 – *Kipper cards*

7 – *Angel cards*

8 – *Geomancy*

9 – *Lenormand cards*

10 – *Dice oracle*

11 – *Power animal cards*

12 – *Dream interpretation*

13 – *Diary / Free writing / automatic writing*

14 – *Jewel or stone oracle*

15 – *Something different*

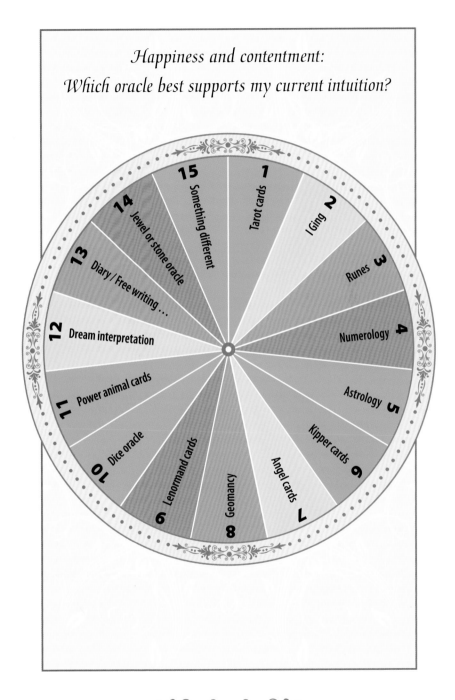

Happiness and contentment:
Which oracle best supports my current intuition?

1 Tarot cards
2 I Ging
3 Runes
4 Numerology
5 Astrology
6 Kipper cards
7 Angel cards
8 Geomancy
6 Lenormand cards
10 Dice oracle
11 Power animal cards
12 Dream interpretation
13 Diary / Free writing …
14 Jewel or stone oracle
15 Something different

Happiness and contentment: Whom can I especially thank for my luck and happiness?

1 – *Partner*
2 – *Lover*
3 – *Daughter*
4 – *Son*
5 – *Mother*
6 – *Father*
7 – *Grandparents*
8 – *Friends*
9 – *Sister*
10 – *Brother*
11 – *Aunt*
12 – *Uncle*
13 – *Godchild, grandson/granddaughter*
14 – *Unknown person*
15 – *Teacher, lecturer*
16 – *Colleague*
17 – *Priest, artist, therapist*
18 – *Father-in-law, mother-in-law*
19 – *Best friend*
20 – *Myself*
21 – *Employer*
22 – *Classmates, fellow students*
23 – *Neighbor*
24 – *Other relatives*
25 – *A "chance encounter"*

Happiness and contentment: Whom can I especially thank for my luck and happiness?

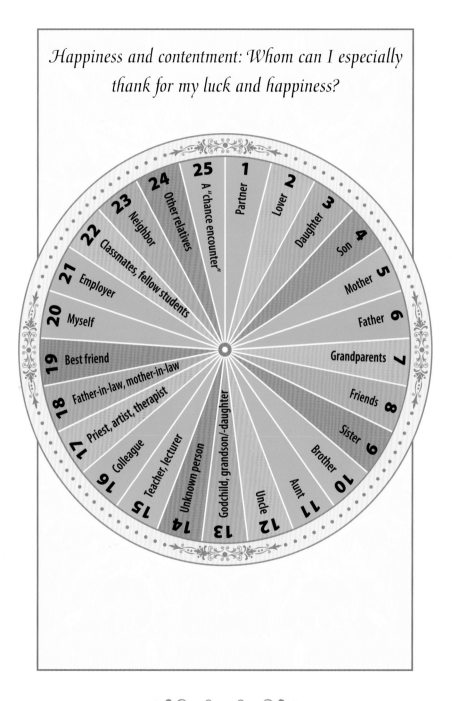

Blank diagrams

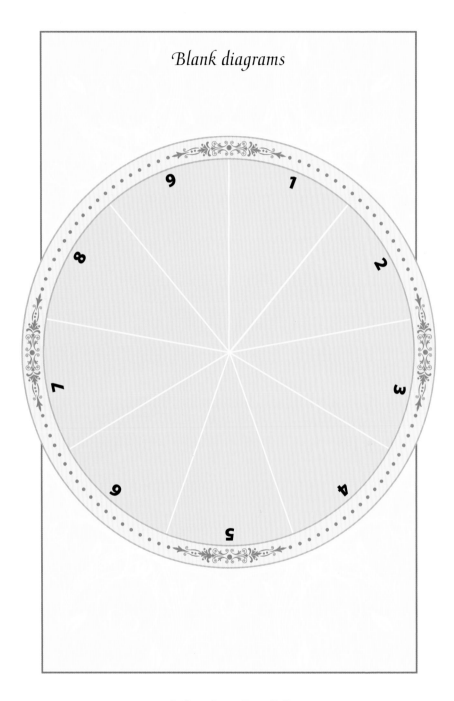

Blank diagrams

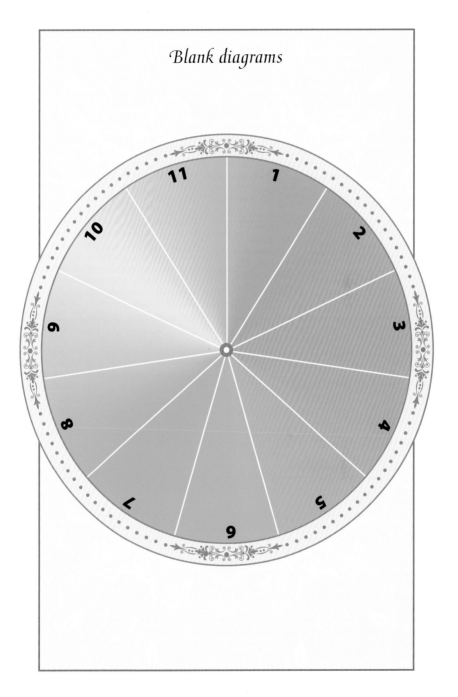

Blank diagrams

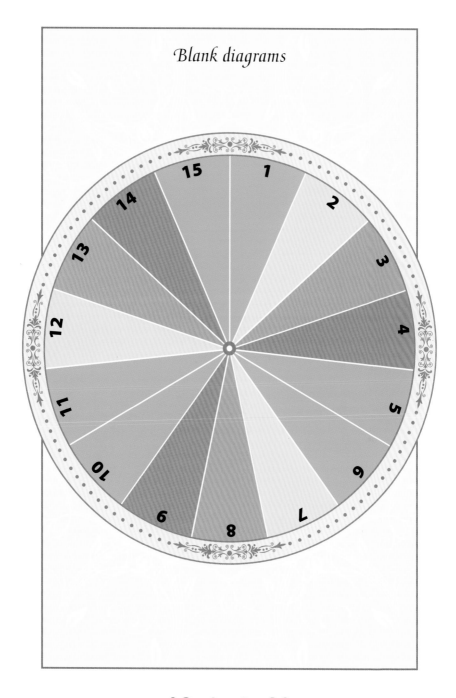

Blank diagrams

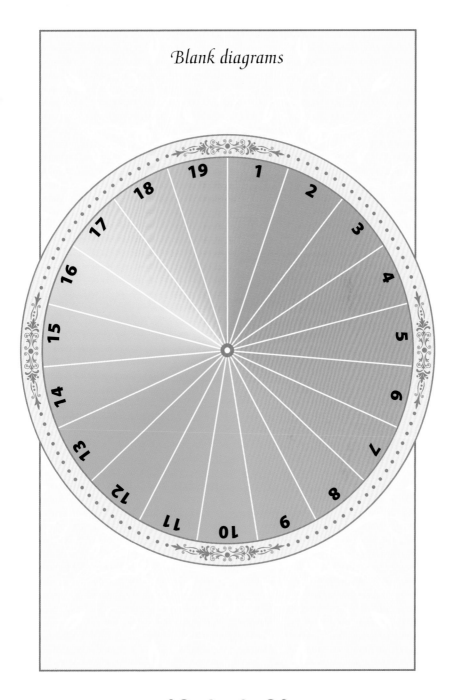

Blank diagrams

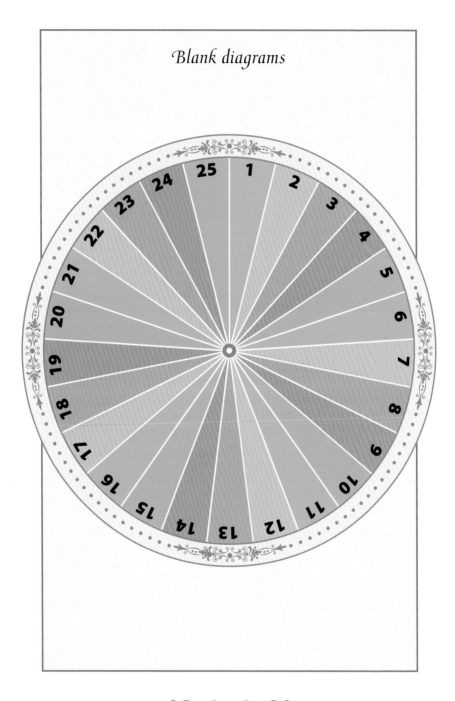

Using the pendulum as an oracle

Ingrid Kraaz von Rohr

Opportunities for a successful life

Most people long for success, recognition and love within their relationship and family, success in their job, health, material independence and security, harmony with the people around them and inner joy and safety. Yet there is much more that we long for and that is important for us.

In real life, things often look different. We find that it is not easy to manage the different aspects of our lives and keep all deadlines. We then find that we are left behind, that we do not get what we deserve. And yet we know so much that things could be changed, and run far more smoothly. However, the last bit of "know how" as to what we should put effort into and how we should implement it is still missing.

And, naturally enough, we first need to find out what is really important for us. What has priority? Which rules should I obey? These things vary from person to person.

Start by loving yourself. This does not mean a kind of egocentric love but something that is really important for you. I have personally noted down a pendulum diagram with the following answers; you may enter these possibilities in this way, or similarly, into the blank pendulum diagrams in this book:

What will help me to focus on what is important?

Meditation
More sleep
Better and healthier food
More body training
More time to sit down and really find out

More confidence in myself
More security and self-esteem
Bach Flowers
The right color as help and therapy

What should I train or learn?
Avoid all distractions
Exercises to increase my self-esteem
Let go of former things
Make decisions more easily
Use my energies right
Find out what I really want
Find out what life asks me to do

What should I care for to live my life fully?
Trust in the creative power
Be authentic
Experience and live maturity
Honesty
Modesty
Let go of the past
Do not think about the future
Live in the present moment

On occasion of his 70th birthday, Charlie Chaplin wrote the following lines about life:

"As I began to love myself I understood that at any circumstance, I am in the right place at the right time, and everything happens at the exactly right moment, so I could be calm.
Today I call it 'self-confidence'.

As I began to love myself I stopped craving for a different life, and I could see that everything that surrounded me was inviting me to grow.
Today I call it 'maturity'.

As I began to love myself I quit steeling my own time, and I stopped designing huge projects for the future. Today, I only do what brings me joy and happiness, things I love to do and that make my heart cheer, and I do them in my own way and in my own rhythm.

Today I call it 'simplicity'.

As I began to love myself I freed myself of anything that is no good for my health – food, people, things, situations, and everything that drew me down and away from myself.

At first I called this attitude a healthy egoism. Today I know it is 'love of oneself'.

As I began to love myself I quit trying to always be right, and ever since I was wrong less of the time.

Today I discovered that is 'modesty'.

As I began to love myself I refused to go on living in the past and worry about the future. Now, I only live for the moment, where everything is happening.

Today I live each day, day by day, and I call it 'fulfillment'.

As I began to love myself I recognized that my mind can disturb me and it can make me sick. But as I connected it to my heart, my mind became a valuable ally.

Today I call this connection 'wisdom of the heart'.

We no longer need to fear arguments, confrontations or any kind of problems with ourselves or others. Even stars collide, and out of their crashing new worlds are born.

Today I know that is 'life'!"

What famous people had to say about this

Many philosophers, mystics, and – interestingly – physicists and Nobel laureates have discovered this force which is in all of us and which takes effect from there.

Max Planck declared in one of his talks: "We must assume that a conscious, intelligent spirit is behind this force. This spirit is the very reason of existence of matter (the outer world). Not the visible (outer) yet transient matter is what is really and truly reality but the invisible, eternal spirit (soul) is what is real."

And **Werner Heisenberg** made it clear in this way: "The first drink from the cup of natural science brings atheism, but at the bottom of the cup waits God."

Max von Laue: "The natural scientists wanted to look directly into the face of God. As this has proved impossible, these exact scientists claimed that HE did not exist. Yet – how much more modest have we natural scientists become. We bow in modesty in front of the super-large, the all-powerful, the eternally invisible which we can never fully comprehend."

Albert Einstein: "The scientists' religious feeling takes the form of rapturous amazement at the harmony of natural law, which reveals an intelligence of such superiority that, compared with it, all the systematic thinking and acting of human beings is an utterly insignificant reflection."

Rajinder Singh writes in his book "Die Weisheit der erwachten Seele": "Our view is limited to the outer world of mind and matter. We are taught from our birth on to engage with the toys of this world. But who teaches us to go inside? Can anybody remember his or her parents or teachers showing him or her how to expand our perception to the untouched side in us? Did anybody ever tell us to become aware of our inner aspects as we grew up? If this never was the case, our attention which is guided by our mind has become used to only regarding the outer world."

Man, know thyself

It has become clear to everybody that times have changed. In other words, the problems we currently face are more clearly and more consciously on the minds of people. Thus, we may more easily formulate questions to receive the answers we need.

The objective, for me, is to learn to act fully consciously and with a determined question and aim in mind. In this New Age it is all about understanding which fruits our actions will bear. Now is the time to change things.

Results as well as decisions are in the hands of every one of us. You may gain liberty and prepare in a relaxed way for the New Age with its unique civilization. You decide whether you prefer the negative or decide to do what is good, ethical, true – the love of the heart that rules all and everything.

The will of God is able to move *all* worlds. The love of God and of every one of us causes and determines what happens.

All this is related to frequencies. In the beginning, we feel these frequencies in our bodies, later we feel them spiritually – in our soul. It is the love that grows. It makes it easier for us to feel the frequencies. The more love grows from a bodily to a spiritual state, the more we will experience creative intuition and creativity.

Yet what we really need is experience. Just imagine that I'd try to explain to you what real chocolate tastes like when you've only tasted cheap chocolate before and did not even know that one can buy real chocolate made of real cacao. How can I explain something I have never experienced or tasted before? You will not become aware of the taste of real chocolate until you've tasted it and let it melt on your tongue. You – in a manner of speaking – become one with the chocolate because your tongue and your other organs of sensation transmit your perception as a state of conscious experience. Reason alone won't manage this. And this is where the use of pendulum makes sense: to sort what is good for you – and what is not.

Everyone can only be what he or she is at this very moment. Each of us possesses our own frequency or form of revelation. But we can

grow – this is what each person intends anyway. Discover your talents and your hidden abilities. Don't let yourself get passed by the wayside by distractions of the outer world. It is time to open up for ethical guidelines. You yourself prepare your own future. So wake up!

Many of us are convinced that we have already awoken and are conscious. Be generous and give love. The more you give it, the more it grows, in contrast to a cup of flour which you might give your neighbor. The love we give increases in giving.

It is important that you understand that it would do us all good if we reached equilibrium to escape from the crossing forces at the crossroads of source and end. This will only happen when you start to change something yourself and go new and ethical ways and follow the love that gives.

The more awareness you develop, the more you will be able to feel the power of your soul – and to use it. It is a special kind of power which lives in each human being and forms him or her and guides them if they are willing to listen and to emphasize.

May each of us focus and unite for the common good of all mankind.

Respect, love and forgiveness are the keys to our progress, to elevate our frequencies. Start with yourself and freely share these attributes with your fellow men. May you experience this power that resides in all of us as soon as possible.

This wish which I hand over to you is the quintessence of all my professional and private experience which I have made using the pendulum (and the Bach Flowers as well as color healing) in the past years and decades. The right frequency heals – and the "right" frequency is the one that hits my basic tone, the source that informs all that I do.

May you enjoy discovering yourself! Discover all that you are able to, what you really want deep in your heart. And don't be satisfied with anything mediocre. Focus on your task. Never give up. There is an old saying, "Never ever give up. There is always hope."

The more you train and learn to be always completely focused on what you do, the better you become, and the more happiness you find in your life. It really pays off.

Become quiet by enjoying concentration. Take part in God's creation by learning to know thyself.

I believe it is no coincidence that you read these words. If you encounter these words today, this is because you have fulfilled all preconditions and understand that not a drop of water falls in this world without cause. Everything is good. May you feel well and live and love with your whole being and become happy. May this book assist you in proceeding on this thrilling path of getting to know yourself.

THE RETURN OF THE ORACLE

HAJO BANZHAF

Whether we have any use for oracles in our time or not, most of all depends on how each individual deals with them. Does one consult the oracle out of weakness or strength? Those who do this out of weakness subdue themselves to the oracle and will not even leave their home in the end if the cards or stars don't "allow" them to. These persons should soon comprehend that Tarot (or any other oracle) is a good servant but a bad master. It can enrich oneself to use the service of an oracle but it is an error to blindly obey it.

Navigation in paradoxical life situations

In addition, some people look at oracles as a form of esoteric guarantee of luck and happiness, that is, a system that ensures everything will go well. However, I have my doubts that we are only in this world to feel well. Quite the contrary: we are here to overcome internal and external tension and contradictions. And this cannot be achieved by avoiding all that is challenging. If we look at a horoscope we find that each of us was born with tension and internal contradictions. It appears as if we are given a lifetime to remodel these dissonances into a great symphony.

Yet there is another temptation when we deal with an oracle which must be resisted by modern man: our wish to receive an unambiguous answer whatever the case. Often enough, the answers are ambiguous or difficult to understand, and they are never certain. There have been many attempts to reduce this ambiguity to unambiguousness. They hark back to the times before the 20th century and are all based on a deterministic world-view. The modern man should be able to comprehend that ambiguity and contradictions bring a highly creative field of tension into being, which would certainly be extinguished by unambiguousness. Carl Jung once said "What is paradox strangely enough is one of our highest spiritual goods; unambiguousness however is a sign of weakness. Only what is paradox can fully embrace the plenty that is life."

How can we explain an oracle?

A term that Carl Jung has coined, synchronicity, sounds good but explains very little. It simply affirms that two things which happen at the same time can be connected in a purposeful way. This is why I here offer two further considerations:

- On the one hand, we have the quality of time, which means that every moment has its own special meaning. On the other hand, a holistic view of the world assumes that question and answer belong together, that they form a whole. If you connect both thoughts it becomes clear that the moment of the question already contains the answer. If we manage to discern the quality of the moment in which we ask a question we can read the answer. And this is what the oracle systems of this world do in their very own way. The astrologer looks up to the stars – or rather in his computer nowadays – in ancient China, the I Ging was thrown, a druid consulted the runes and the Tarot practitioner questions the cards. All the oracles mirror the quality of the moment in their picture or symbolic language and in this give an answer to the question posed. None of these systems is superior to any other. What is important is that the interpreter understands its language.

- There is another very interesting consideration which doubts the source of the knowledge in the "depth", in our unconsciousness. We often talk about the unconscious as if it were our private property which we carry around with us. But no one can tell us where it is located and how far it may reach. It is possible that it is limitless; maybe it connects us to eternity.

Part of a greater whole

As a comparison, think of a wave that is connected to the depth of the ocean. This wave is a symbol of our personal nature. The surf where it breaks represents our consciousness while the dark towering wave stands for our personal unconsciousness and the ocean for the collective unconsciousness to which all waves and all individuals are connected. In the same way, our consciousness may be connected to the greater whole at all times. Teilhard de Chardin called this the noosphere (from the Greek *nous* = spirit) which envelops earth as a collective consciousness in which we all participate.

We have all had an experience when thoughts that suddenly arise seemingly out of nowhere are far better than ideas we have considered for a long time. But where does the origin of these wonderful insights lie? Obviously, our consciousness is wired to the sphere of the spirit. This is confirmed by the neuroscientist and Nobel laureate Sir John Eccles who says, "Our brain does not produce energy, it receives it." We do not realize this possibility because – metaphorically spoken – the frequencies had to be reduced in order for us to "disconnect" our consciousness so we can experience ourselves as an I, as an identity.

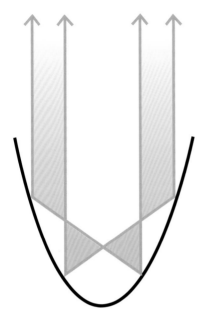

Another very visual symbol for this connectedness is the parable. If you send signals from its focal point they will be reflected in such a way that they beam into the infinite as parallels. But geometry teaches us that these parallels will intersect there – even if we cannot imagine just how. And this means that a parable has a focal point in this world and a second one in the infinite. Both are always connected like our Ego with our higher Self.

And this leads us back to the point where we started: even if we no longer hear the voices of the gods and goddesses because our consciousness has evolved so much, we are in a constant connection with them – or our higher Self.

I believe that it won't be long until we understand that three concepts we feel today that are hardly connected do describe exactly the same. These concepts are coincidence, destiny and unconsciousness. It appears as if our unconsciousness created situations, opportunities, encounters, and experiences which we perceive as coincidence and which – in the best sense – will make up our destiny. Oracles assist us to better understand what sense such coincidences have.

Taken from: Hajo Banzhaf, Die Rückkehr der Orakel; from the book Hajo Banzhaf: Zwischen Himmel und Erde. Die Quintessenz aus Esoterik, Astrologie and Tarot. ISBN 9783868265224, p. 139 ff.

Pendulum: Oracle, Advice, Self-Help

This edition published by Shelter Harbor Press by arrangement with Alexian Ltd.

Shelter Harbor Press
603 W. 115th Street
Suite 163
New York, NY 10025

For sales in North America and UK, please contact
info@shelterharborpress.com

Picture credits
All images included in this volume are in the public domain, with the exception of the following, for whom the publishers gratefully acknowledge permissions:

Cover design: Jessica Quistorff in use of the images from fotolia.com "Magic book" © Ivan Bliznetsov and "beauty frame" © aalto
Images: p. 8 "The Universe" from the Original Aleister Crowley Thoth Tarot © Ordo Templi Orientis / AGM AGMüller Urania – p. 10: Wikipedia: pendulum of Foucault in the Orangerie, Kassel /Germany – p. 24: Fotolia.com, Magic pendulum © Photosani – p. 31: Fotolia.com, astrologer © Photosani – p. 154: Fotolia.com, Wave © Felipe Oliveira – p. 154: Parabola by Hermann Betken and Hajo Banzhaf
Book design: Jessica Quistorff and Antje Betken; ornaments by Hermann Betken in use of the image from fotolia.com "beauty frame" © aalto
Typesetting, artwork, image selection: Antje Betken

Original German Edition: © 2011 by Koenigsfurt-Urania Verlag GmbH,

Cataloging-in-Publication Data has been applied for and may be obtained from the Library of Congress

ISBN: 978-1-62795-020-6

Printed and bound in China

10 9 8 7 6 5 4 3 2 1

Sources

Ideas, inspiration, and texts were taken with kind permission from the following sources: **Susanne Peymann: Pendeln – Liebe, Glück, Erfolg.** Krummwisch, 4th ed. 2010 (KönigsfurtUrania). | **Johannes Fiebig: Die Schönheit der Bewegung.** Anmerkungen zu Psychologie and Praxis des Pendeln, in: Susanne Peymann: Pendeln – Liebe, Glück, Erfolg. ibid. | **Johannes Fiebig: Das Unsichtbare sichtbar machen.** Orakel heute and das tägliche Wunder. unpublished manuscript. | **Roberto Gadini: Pendeln – Macht and Magie.** Turin 2005 (Lo Scarabeo / KönigsfurtUrania).

Notes: p. 8: Text on the Crowley Tarot: E. Bürger / J. Fiebig: *Tarot Basics Crowley.* Krummwisch 2009 (KönigsfurtUrania). | **p. 9 f.:** Sleep as "different room" and awakening in a room that appears to be unknown, based on Christian Kellerer: *Der Sprung ins Leere. Objet trouvé. Surrealismus. Zen.* Köln 1986 (Du-Mont). | *p. 12 f.:* Wikipedia German: lemma " Radiästhesie". | **p. 14 f.:** Pluto as double god etc., and **p. 17,** subterranean water vein: cf. Johannes Fiebig: *Der Skorpion in uns. Geheimnis and Leidenschaft.* Krummwisch 1990 (Königsfurt). | p. 15: transition Aquarius–Pisces based on Johannes Fiebig: *Die Fische in uns. Glaube and Vertrauen.* Krummwisch 1991 (Königsfurt). | **p. 17:** cf. Frederik Hetmann / Hans-Christian Kirsch: *Von einem, der auszog, das Fürchten zu lernen. Märchen sammeln, erzählen, deuten.* J. Fiebig, ed. Krummwisch 2004 (Königsfurt-Urania). | **p. 21 f.:** cf. Sigmund Freud: *Selbstdarstellung* [1924] and *Kurzer Abriss der Psychoanalyse* [1923], in: Freud: *Selbstdarstellung. Schriften zur Geschichte der Psychoanalyse.* Frankfurt a.M. 1971 (S. Fischer), p. 69 – 72, 207 f. | **p. 22:** Julia Cameron: *Der Weg des Künstlers: Ein spiritueller Pfad zur Aktivierung unserer Kreativität.* Munich, new edition 2009 (Knaur). original: *The Artist's Way. A Spiritual Path to Higher Creativity.* Tarcher; 1st ed. 1992 | *p. 23:* André Breton: *Die Manifeste des Surrealismus.* different edition, f.e. Reinbek 1986 (rororo). US-edition: *Manifestoes of Surrealism.* University of Michigan Press 1969 | **p. 26:** Michael Lemster, in: *BuchJournal,* Winter 2004. | **p. 146 f.:** Charlie Chaplin on his 70th birthday, quoted after *Natur & Heilen* 12/2009; American original quoted after www.free-meditation.ca/archives/482.

About the authors

Bestselling author Susanne Peymann (who has sold more than 80,000 books about oracles) manages to provide a unique bridge between the traditional esoteric approach, and modern day psychology. She presents old and contemporary pendulum tables to provide practical support in today's world of constant decision making.

This book includes an original contribution by Ingrid Kraaz von Rohr on *Using the Pendulum as an Oracle* and an excerpt from Hajo Banzhaf's *The Return of the Oracle*.